PRETTY PERSONAL

GEORGE DAUGIRD

PRETTY PERSONAL

SPHERE BOOKS LIMITED

Sphere Books Limited, 27 Wrights Lane, London W8 5TZ

First published in Great Britain in 1987 by Sphere Books Ltd
Copyright © 1987 by George Daugird

TRADE
MARK

Set in Palatino by
Rowland Phototypesetting Ltd
Bury St Edmunds, Suffolk

Printed and bound in Great Britain by
Cox and Wyman Ltd, Reading, Berks

CONTENTS

AUTHOR'S NOTE

To everyone who has ever placed a personal ad or intends to do so. Thanks . . . for sharing. Whoever you are, wherever you are, I love each and every one of you.

P.S. These ads are as genuine as the persons standing behind them.

From the beginning of time, man has been searching. One day, in the Garden of Eden, Adam tore off a papyrus leaf from an overhanging branch and began to write:

Young man,
179 years old,
blue eyes and blond hair,
single and in possession of a camel,
is looking for . . .

Stumped, unable to complete the world's first personal, he dropped his Parker pen and rubbed his chin. He knew he was searching for something but he wasn't exactly sure what that something was. Or that it was a who.

Fortunately for Adam, God answered his prayers. Eve was created and we all know the rest of the story.

Turning a few years ahead, we discover the world really hasn't changed all that much after countless centuries of 'progress'. Our modern day 'Adams' – perhaps more fully if not better dressed than Adam Senior and driving a Rover instead of a camel – are still dissatisfied, still a little confused and still searching for that someone who will make them complete. And, in many ways, it is like looking for a needle in a haystack.

INTRODUCTION

On the other hand, the world HAS changed since Adam and Eve first bit into an apple. Iron 'curtains' and nuclear 'umbrellas', acid rain and a 'Cold' War, test-tube babies and millions and millions 'on the dole' – sometimes you don't know whether to laugh . . . or to cry! If only Adam had known where his papyrus leaf would lead to, he might have thought twice and saved us from ourselves.

But unfortunately he didn't. And now, thanks to him, we have a real mess on our hands. Not only are there Adams looking for Eves . . . but also Eves looking for Adams. And if that isn't bad enough, we have Adams looking for Adams and Eves looking for Eves and some Adams teamed up with Eves looking for an Adam (or an Eve, or both) and some who are only interested in apples, apparently, and one dog who is looking for . . . well, you'll find out. They are all there – and more! – in the pages to come. People searching for The One True Love. A life partner. A regular – or sometimes not so 'regular' – contact. Or someone just to talk to. You name it, there's an ad for it.

A selection of these personals is collected here for your amusement and pleasure. No special claim is made as to their uniqueness or originality even though some are quite funny, even witty. Nor is any guarantee given that you will be touched in the same way as others have been by the messages conveyed. Like anything in life, that's up to you!

CHAPTER 1 ■■■

SEX

Sex is quite often the first thing that comes to mind when someone mentions 'personals' or 'contact ads'. That isn't so strange, given our current pre-occupation with sex in our daily life. Yet remarkably the personals of today are proportionately less sexy than the ads of, say, ten years ago. This in part is a result of the contact ads gaining greater legitimacy as an acceptable means of initiating contact with others. Consequently, leaving aside for the moment the overtly sexy magazines and newspapers, less than twenty to twenty-five per cent of today's ads are explicitly aimed at sex.

Someone once said – it must have been an American – that the average Brit makes love once a week . . . and that's why the streets in London are so deserted on a Sunday morning. But he was simply jealous. Jealous of the sex clubs, jealous of the bordellos, jealous of our 'topless' newspapers and jealous of a relaxed open-minded-ness towards sex. Most of all, he was probably jealous of the guy next to him at work, sitting at his desk, bent over, pretending to be working on

9

something. Whatever his neighbour was working on, you might find right here.

Contrary to what many foreigners may think, the British are the sexiest people in the world. Even worse than the Eskimos who, as you know . . .

But that's another story.

For now, rather than saving the best for last, let's begin with . . .

An E for erotic.

Buddhists swear that erotic behaviour is a wonderful source of inspiration and energy. I agree with this sentiment wholeheartedly and would like to meet a woman who would also like to bring more erotic elements into play in her life. I am both active and easy-going, introverted and extroverted and my tennis isn't bad. And you?

Young man seeks broad-minded girlfriend for a cozy, erotic relationship.

Musician, built in 1951 with crab licence plates
(ergo, romantic and artistic), likes to snuggle in
shows, theatres, parks and museums and would
like to meet an attractive, loving and erotic woman
up to 35 years.

HONEST IS HONEST

I am looking for a fine, exciting, erotic relationship
with a fun woman. I am a man of 33, not
unattractive and tender . . . although I may wish
to rip your clothes off.

The lessons of Don Juan. Which woman would
like to escape the daily boredom by having an
exciting, erotic adventure with a not unattractive
man of 28? Who dares?

Stop here, you radiant, beautiful sexy girl with a
rich inner life. You go for high heels and exotic
clothes and look on life as an excellent opportunity
to realize your wishes. You are looking for me – a
good-looking guy of 25, a physicist and musician
bursting with other talents – in order to experience
'the erotic' and other adventures. A letter plus a
photo are all you need to start a fabulous new
phase in your life.

Are you an intelligent young woman who enjoys
erotic things? Let's do something together with
our fantasies.

Man, 48, physical therapist, married to a woman
invalid, would like to meet a woman for a fine
erotic relationship.

Unattached man, just turned 40, a bit dominant, desires a fast, playful young woman with huge breasts and an interest for provocative lingerie and all that is erotic.

Good-for-nothing guy seeks a tough gal for playful, adventuresome, erotic contact.

Good-looking, fresh and healthy young guy of 25 seeks the same in a girl/woman, purely for an erotic relation. I surprise myself at my own daring! You don't necessarily have to have a 'relation' just to be able to make good love. I am very trustworthy and am not an adventurer. Do you dare? Respond if necessary anonymously (only with your telephone number) but do enclose a photo.

Pipe-smoking man of 35, attached, seeks an (un)attached intelligent woman with a sense of humour who just like him has a need for good conversation and erotic adventure.

Unattached man of 37, a bit shy, seeks girlfriend mainly for an erotic relation.

For some time I have hesitated, but still . . . Young man of 34 who enjoys humour and passion is looking for a like-minded woman, up to 45. Purpose: to get together once or more per month and give life more erotic content.

There is room within my regular relationship for a casual erotic contact with an intelligent, blond woman (preferably also unattached). The person behind this ad is a psychiatrist.

Thin man seeks woman of an independent nature for an exciting, erotic contact.

Extremely handsome young man, good position, honest and trustworthy, would like to indulge women by satisfying their wildest erotic desires. Preferably during the day. No financial intentions.

If you are a submissive woman who enjoys fantasy and an erotic-filled love life, then write to me, a man of 32.

A fine loving woman for a friendly and erotic relationship. That is what I would like to have, a man of 34. Making love can indeed be good when there is respect and appreciation for each other.

▼▼▼▼▼▼

If you don't find what you want under E, then you can always try S for sensual – or sensuous.

I am NOT looking for a permanent relation. Rather, contact with a woman, every now and then. I am an attractive man of 32. I am sensual and I seek sensual.

Which woman would like to learn the art of sensual massage at the hands of a 40-year-old man?

Man seeks sensuous woman in order to make tender love.

Which well-off, sensual woman would like to make her sex fantasies come true with a good-looking 40-year-old attached man?

Lovable woman of 38 seeks sensuous man for making love and friendship.

Desired: a sensual woman in order for her to experience some exciting things with a soft, beautiful man of 33.

For only the price of a postage stamp you – a SENSUAL woman – can get in touch with me, a sensual man of 34.

If erotic and sensual are not your cup of tea, then look for another popular adjective, 'intimate', preferably in combination with 'relation(ship)'. And, failing everything else, you can go for broke and look quite bluntly for 'sex(ual)' – again often in combination with 'relation(ship)'.

Young man of 20 seeks woman up to 42 for intimate relationship.

Student of 21 seeks young woman for tender and free sexual relation.

Good-looking guy seeks Negress – thin, fat, chubby, doesn't matter, age unimportant – for sex relationship.

14

Are you a sexily dressed woman? Trim young man of 26 desires you for an adventuresome evening by candlelight.

Man of 39, ardent lover, seeks uninhibited sex relationship without taboos with a young attractive woman. Discretion assured and desired.

Young blond man seeks sex correspondence and sex relation with a woman who can receive at home.

I feel myself attracted to older women. This is why I am seeking contact with an older woman up to age 55 for an unconstrained sexual relation. I am a sporty man of 23.

Sensual leather boy seeks the same in a leather girl up to 25 for a ski vacation and eventually a permanent (sex) relationship.

Doctor seeks girlfriend between ages 20 and 35 for intimate relationship, visits to 'pair' clubs and so forth.

Man of 33 is looking for free and easy sex contact with women between the ages 18 to 55. I am crazy about really big women with broad, robust and solid bodies. Preferably unattached. A sense of style, hygiene, humour appreciated. I myself cannot receive at home. Always an answer.

Rich young man of 36 seeks sexy girl of 18 to 24.

Modest, bashful and honourable student seeks sexual relation with a friendly woman.

A giant of a man, 48, seeks a plump woman with huge breasts for a cozy, intimate and steady relationship.

Man of 37 would like an intimate relationship with a handicapped woman.

Nice guy, well hung, very hot, seeks well-endowed woman up to 50 years for sexual relation. Responses with photos, please. Serious reactions will receive a picture of a naked nice man.

New inspiration for a new year. Young man seeks girlfriend(s) to laugh together, to make love together, and to do all sorts of fun things . . . together. Casual sex, a romantic affair, living apart together (LAT). Who knows?

Man of 27 would like to meet a woman who in order to spur her own 'growth' would like to dig deeper into TANTRA/SEX/MEDITATION.

▼▼▼▼▼▼

By now you're erotic, feeling sensual and primed for an intimate sexual relationship. But in order to 'make love', you'll still need one half of the sexual coin. The first half is called, quite appropriately: lover.

Are you a woman who would like very much to enjoy having a young lover of 22? Don't hesitate . . . WRITE!

Man of 29 seeks a woman lover. Why? Because I love it!

Fun-loving man of 31 seeks fun-loving woman lover of around 25. You like to stroll along the beach and through the woods, bicycle, enjoy good food, wine and a pleasant chat.

Ugly-looking SOB, impossible to live with but as a lover top-rate, is looking for a no-strings-attached relationship with a breathtakingly beautiful, voluptuous woman in order for both of us to give free reign to our basic desires and perverse lusts. Which shameless Messalina dares to take up the challenge?

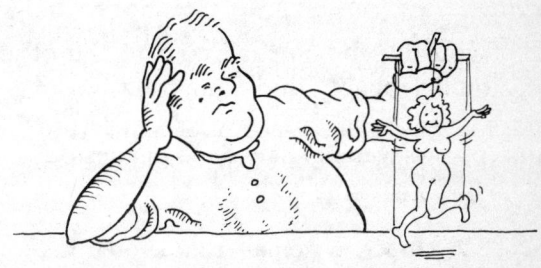

I am a good LOVER. Which woman between 40 and 55 would like to find this out first hand?

An arm around you. Your head on my shoulder. Sporty, blond man of 35 seeks spontaneous, attractive woman to whom I can be a man, a friend and a lover.

Passion and romance sought in the form of a lover by an attached woman.

CHALLENGE. The man of your life and a pleasant job awaits you. Which charming young lady, a lover of life, will pick up the glove? I am a sensitive experienced man of 48 and I know how to please a woman as a lover. Write me in confidence.

FAT is BEAUTIFUL, exciting and erotic. I have a fine, steady relationship and I shall never give her up. But if you are a fun, amply endowed woman who is looking for a tender and fiery lover, here I am. All you have to do is grab a pen and write me a letter.

▼▼▼▼▼▼

And if you flip the 'sexual' coin to the other side, you'll probably find a mistress.

The fireplace is waiting. Man seeks mistress for long winter evenings.

WANTED: Attractive woman from 18 on up as mistress for two to three hours per day. Excellent net monthly salary and beautiful apartment in cheerful surroundings. For an unattached, very busy manager of 30.

Exciting, isn't it? Married man, 34, seeks a mistress for during the day.

THE LONGING. Oh, oh, those men. They always want to go further, they always want more, something different, something exciting . . . Or do such women also exist? I, a man of 32, am looking for a mistress to fill the gaps.

An intelligent, sensitive and muscular 40-year-old married man, of strong character and body, seeks a mistress.

Finally, there are those who leave little room for doubt about what it's all about. It's about 'making love' and 'going to bed'.

I am a 31-year-old man, not married, hard of hearing and who would like to make love. Due to my handicap I have problems with making contacts with, for example, prostitutes (by telephone). This is why I would like to enter a confidential relationship with a loving girl or woman. Age and skin colour are not important. I am sentimental and romantic and love music.

Are you the woman who is ready, willing and able to make love to a prim man in his forties? Yes, making love . . . but that doesn't include a trip to City Hall first.

Thiry-four-year-old has time for smart teenagers who would like to philosophize – or make love – with a somewhat older guy.

Man seeks woman who is willing to really fondle and make love.

Man of 46, teaching at university, would like to 'really make love' after eight years of total abstinence.

Man of 51 would like to go to bed a couple times with a woman of roughly the same age.

Long-lasting love sessions. Being friends . . . but without obligations. Man of 37, strong personality, seeks woman with the same wishes.

Why not? Without complications, every now and then GOING TO BED with a young-looking guy of 42. Which young woman dreams of this?

An easy-going guy of 34 invites you, a fast lady, to be (un)usually sweet for each other: kissing and making love as well as drinking beer and eating (out). Now a reaction from your side, please.

Guy with a fine body seeks women who want to make love.

Young man seeks girl who can laugh, bicycle and make love.

▼▼▼▼▼▼

As you might have guessed by now, there are any number of words which are suggestive of the advertiser's ultimate intentions. Two words that send out warnings at an early stage are 'married' and 'attached'.

Married man seeks girlfriend.

Attached man would like to visit you – a sexy woman – ever so often in order to fill his emptiness . . . and hopefully hers, too!

There could be any number of good reasons why you, an attached woman, just as I, an attached man of 41, would be looking for a serious and open friendship. I guarantee that your reaction will be handled with the fullest discretion.

Extroverted young housewife, definitely not a pro, is looking for regular contact with a proper and well-off gentleman.

Friendly guy seeks girlfriend in order to make love with the support of an open and loving comradeship. This with the approval of my spouse.

I am an attractive woman of 35 looking with the knowledge of my husband for a friend in order to go out and, if it 'clicks', to do that other 'thing'. No problem if you are attached.

Man of 30 is seeking without the knowledge of his girlfriend contact with a bisexual woman/girl or a sensual lesbian couple. For contact/relationship.

Attractive, healthy, attached man is seeking with permission of spouse a girlfriend up to the age of 40 for many fine evenings by you at home.

Another group not known to raise eyebrows – except in this company – are the businessmen. Then again, who else knows better the added value of advertising?

Due to erotic shortcomings an attached businessman of 48 is seeking a proper lady between 35 and 40 for whom the erotic is an important link in her life and who also feels she is missing out. A hundred per cent discretion assured. Only serious letters with recent photo will be answered.

Businessman, 44 years old, seeks loving, servile woman up to 60 years for an erotic relationship without taboos. Making love = pleasure for two.

Attractive and rich director of a company, 44 and married, is looking for a young woman to take good care of and to go on business trips together.

Married businessman, 41, easy-going, would like to meet an attractive young woman for a complementary relationship.

Married businessman, 40, a 'teddy bear', desires a romantic and erotic girlfriend. No problems if she is attached.

▼▼▼▼▼▼

Something that is striking is that those advertising for sex are an extremely discreet group. Why else would this be emphasised in ad after ad?

If you are a woman who gets excited at the idea of an 'erotic' phone call, then please respond. I am a 45-year-old man and believe that respect for each other and discretion are preconditions to such a contact.

You have everything. A loving man, healthy kids, vacations overseas. Still, you wonder sometimes, where is the vibration? The tingling of the unexpected? The tension and butterflies in the stomach? Life is more . . . it doesn't have to slip through your fingers. You are also obviously looking for more; otherwise you wouldn't be reading this section of the paper. If you desire this added dimension to life, then please respond. I am a man who is seeking you, a vibrant and exotic woman up to age 33. Discretion is assured.

Ardent man massages, caresses and makes love to women. No financial reimbursement expected. Discretion absolutely assured!

Sympathetic and experienced dominant man of 36 is willing to assist a submissive, masochistic woman to make her wildest erotic fantasies come true. This within a trusting and comfortable setting. Discretion assured.

Speaking of dominance and submission, bondage and S&M, for those who enjoy the original 'kinks' there are plenty to choose from.

Young man has earned some hard slaps for his naked buttocks and seeks a young woman who will give him just that.

Which dominatrix would like a 48-year-old slave for some fun and games?

My fantasy: A woman ties me down and 'does' everything to me (so long as it isn't painful). Who would like to carefully investigate this aspect of my sexuality? I am a 39-year-old man.

Which dominant woman would enjoy using and abusing a man of 30 ever so often to each other's satisfaction?

Dominant man is looking for a girlfriend with a receptive behind.

Lingerie, submission, willingness to be (mis)used. Extremely attractive man seeks beautiful, classy chic who also fantasizes about these same things.

Man in possession of rope and an unbelievable tongue seeks many-sided woman with versatile feet. Are you also interested in erotic S&M?

What should you do with S&M leanings? Does S&M really lead to happiness? Man of 31 would like to talk and experiment with a woman, sadist or masochist, it doesn't matter which.

Are you an attractive woman who dreams of being tied down, abused and similar fantasies? Don't leave it simply at that . . . WRITE ME!

Young, independent woman in possession of a vivacious husband who, unfortunately, has become powerless due to his obsession with bondage. If you are a woman from a good background who would like to enter an unusual friendship while enjoying a man whenever you wish, write me!

I am a man of 34 who is charming and elegant and gentle while making love. But sometimes I like to really dominate. I also get off on wild, emancipated women with a feel for MASOCHISM. Everyone has at some time deserved to be punished. With a whip, for example. I have a good job and am free to receive you in my spacious house.

Tough guy seeks sexy dominant woman or a perverse woman instructor in leather for my 're-education' in soft S&M. I badly need a good spanking, a whip and forced sex.

It's not as easy as it used to be to get a good spanking. Who would like to lend a hand?

What excites me? A ship to live and sail on. My hands tied behind my back. And you on stiletto heels. Which woman would like to go sailing?

The Story of O. Are you a masochistic woman who dreams of erotic games filled to the brim with excitement while acting out one's fantasies? If you are, then you're ready to meet a somewhat unusual guy.

Dominant man seeks masochistic woman who gets off on bizarre clothing, bondage, posing and soft S&M. Discretion offered. Goal: serious relation or marriage. Skin colour unimportant; children welcome.

After S&M and bondage there is the 'fetish' crowd. Those who believe in different strokes for different folks.

Young man will gladly strip and pose naked for men/women.

Young man with a good body would like to meet a fun woman for friendship and an intimate relationship. I am also prepared to give a masturbation show to one or more ladies at their request.

Man seeks transvestite who loves black lingerie.

Guy of 33 looking for an exciting couple. My hobbies are mini-skirts, make-up, super high boots and stiletto heels.

Transvestite with many interests seeks fellow transvestite (please, no gays) to get together ever so often and have a party. I can receive, occasionally.

I am a man fascinated by bestiality and am looking for an honest, spontaneous woman who can help me beyond my fantasies.

26

Transvestite in rubber clothing would like to pose for artists.

Young man would like to find out if he is submissive while dressed up in sexy women's clothes. Which woman is willing to help him find out?

Man would like to be dressed and made up as a woman by a woman or a transvestite.

Of course, some people are happy just to watch.

Which woman enjoys to play voyeuristic games? Young man of 30 would like to talk to her.

Desired: Married couple willing to do 'IT' while young man watches.

Which young woman would get a 'kick' out of watching a man masturbate? You can join me, if you want.

Which couple would find it exciting to be watched during their love-making by a loving blond boy?

On the other hand, there are those who believe every 'picture' tells a story.

Photographer desires contact with (married) couple.

Which young bisexual woman would like to help us make some erotic photos and videos in a relaxed environment?

Young photographer seeks nude models (women) for serious experimental photography.

Video hobbyist offers attractive remuneration to an adventurous woman who would not mind posing (naked) for him. No publication/distribution intended.

Attractive, sensual male exhibitionist is available for nude photography. At the same time I am looking for women's clubs interested in a masturbation show. I am willing to perform on location.

▼▼▼▼▼▼

Although by now one might imagine that everything under the sun has been done – and indeed it has – there are still those who have yet to do it under the sun. Or anywhere, for that matter. A refreshing oasis in a desert of scorched sex.

Inexperienced young man seeks mature woman (age 28 and older) for sex initiation.

Which young woman would like to give lessons in love to an honest man?

Young man, still wet behind the ears, would like to meet a woman who will teach him all she knows about love and sex.

A soft and intelligent man would like to learn how to make love well. Which woman would like to help me along the way?

Attractive guy, well-built but bashful, would like a woman to educate him in the game of the erotic.

Young man seeks experienced lover who is ready, willing and able to teach him everything he ever wanted to know about sex . . . but was afraid to ask.

Bashful, inexperienced man seeks one or maybe two girlfriends who are willing to initiate him into the mysteries of love-making.

A phenomenon not really involving sex *per se* but still requiring some sexual contact is that pertaining to men as 'donors' and women as surrogate mothers. In today's society, almost anything seems possible!

Man would like to have a child and would like to meet a woman willing to be the mother.

Woman would like to meet a good-looking hetero or homosexual male who would like to be the biological father of my first child, with shared responsibility. Only serious reactions, please, along with reasons.

Good-looking fellow, father of four wonderful kids, wishes to make himself available as a donor to a childless married couple or a young woman. I have blond hair, blue eyes and an athletic build.

Do you wish to be a DONOR? I would like to have a child, together with my girlfriend, through self-insemination. I would like to find a donor who would like to remain available later on.

After a five-year relation which suddenly came to an end with a woman to whom I gave four kids, I would like to meet an uninhibited woman for a discreet relation, possibly with me as a donor. This could also be arranged for on an anonymous basis.

I am looking for a FATHER. A man who would be the biological father of my child and would spend roughly 50% of the time with him or her. I am a 38-year-old woman and work four days a week. I currently have a relation with another woman, also a mother. I believe the following to be important traits in a father: playfulness, caring, intelligence, sportive and socially engaged.

Finally, there are those ads which are, well, so special they tend to stand in a class all by themselves. Some are hinting at the obvious. Others seem to be happy simply to be hinting. See if you can figure them out.

Young woman is looking for a policeman with a night stick.

Attractive young man, different than all the others, is looking for a truly beautiful woman who is both whorish and perverse and (at the same time) tasteful and enterprising. For excitement, variation, pleasure and love.

Sexy female hitchhiker sought by a fun man with a fast auto.

Help! Man with sexual problems seeks understanding woman. Purpose: sexual therapy . . . not a relationship!

Overly sensitive post-puberal psychologist would like to meet with a mentally but more importantly physically dominating woman.

Which woman up to the age of 40 would like to spend the whole night together with me, a student?

Do you think you're not 'marketable'? Do you long for a guy who's got everything? Then try me . . . but only if you're a well-endowed and complete woman in every sense of the word.

Man seeks woman with unshaven armpits and big breasts.

Woman on the 'plump' side seeks a playful, serious and engaging friend who is also penetrating. Macho is fine. What do I want? Quite simply, THAT! The rest rises or falls with THAT. Mobility is a precondition; a long breath, too. Those who only last a day can crawl up my back (but only figuratively speaking).

Caressable man of 51 seeks young woman for own personal use.

It's too cold to run around naked outside. Better to be naked in bed and keep each other warm as toast. I am looking for a woman to pop into my toaster.

Man would like to play with fire. Which woman would like to join me?

▼▼▼▼▼▼

There is one ad, however, that says it all. It doesn't beat around the bush. No, it jumps right in.

Young man seeks nymphomaniacs up to 45 years old for a sexual relation. Possibility for either living together or marriage. Handicapped and invalids are also welcome.

CHAPTER 2

Man has traditionally been the Hunter. Clutching a spear, a sword or a rifle in one hand, his 'courage' with the other, he was expected to go out, track down and bring back his prey. This was the ultimate test of his manhood and the skills of pursuit – the Hunt – carried over into his relations with the 'weaker sex'.

But being a hunter has never been easy . . . and it gets harder all the time. In prehistoric times man had only to leave his cave, strangle a sabre-toothed tiger with his bare hands and drag his conquest back to camp by the tail. Nowadays, however, it's a lot worse! A man is actually expected to go out and find work. Not only that but nine times out of ten the dishes are waiting for him when he comes home. Yes, life was much easier back then; now it has become close to being impossible.

And when it comes to 'hunting' down a woman, our modern-day Adam has it far more difficult than his namesake of yesteryear. The first Adam was lucky: he didn't even know he wanted a woman. Compare that to

MAN SEEKS WOMAN

today's man, assaulted from all sides by hundreds, if not thousands of female images. Everyone from Mrs Thatcher and Lady Di on the tube to the latest piece of cheesecake on the cover of Playboy. Is it any wonder that many men, confronted with an unnerving choice of so many women, have exchanged the stone-age club for the ease of pen put to paper?

Man the Hunter has nevertheless retained some claim to this title. On any given weekend, in any given paper, his ads usually outnumber those of women looking for men by two or even three to one. His search is unrelenting, as you will see from the following selection of juicy and tantalising ads.

▼▼▼▼▼▼

Some men choose to be poetic, philosophical or simply 'cute'.

Man with a past and without any money seeks woman without a past and with money.

Thirty-year-old cuddly bear is looking for a girlfriend for more than just 'cuddling'.

I am the world. Savage and treacherous. If you take me on, I'll take you on. Physically I'm a guy, young and attractive. Mentally I am a mountain of force and an ocean full of tenderness. I am the passion, the silence and the love. If you are a young woman and if you understand me, then I will understand you and I long to meet you.

A magician and a romantic with a soothing voice
and a willing ear. If you can't fall asleep at night,
then you should try phoning me. Any time.
Between ten and twelve. Until then, sweet dreams.

If you
want to do more things together
are a woman
have a sense of humour
like Vivaldi
have kid(s)
are politically to the left
like to go camping
exude warmth
wear jeans
are a feeling person
own a bicycle
live with your body
love literature
then there are points we have in common.
I am a man, 44, a father, with a good job and fun
plans.

DESPERATELY SEEKING YOU. Young man seeks
hip gal for going out with and for around the
house.

LOVE
Love is being together. An arm around you. Love
is never more being alone. Love is the sun, the
clouds, the wind. Love is playing like a child. If
this appeals to you, a romantic woman of 35, then
grab a pen, quick, and write me, a divorced man of 39.

Man would like to see his very being and essence
reflected in the eyes and soul of a woman. Let's be
soft for each other, okay?

Prague – Paris – Edinburgh . . . the most beautiful,
the most loving, the most furious, the most tender,
the most sensitive woman in the whole wide
world. Yes . . . this is whom I seek. Crying,
laughing. Running along the beach. From comic
books to Kafka, classical to jazz, Fassbinder to
Romy Schneider. Wild boar meat washed down
with the reddest of wines. I am a Lion and I love
flowers, the colour blue and maybe, just maybe,
You!

And I seek
A girlfriend
And I am a Jewish man.

A small and ugly man desires contact with a pretty
young woman who would like to be treated in
such a way that the SECRETS of the world hidden
within her may be revealed. Let the words come
slowly. In confidence. In surrender. In this way
you will witness the beginning, the birth of your
story.

JAMES BOND would like to take it a little easier
and withdraw into his White Castle. Everything is
available that a woman might want. And, who
knows, he may just have THE role for you in his
latest 007 production.

At the beginning of my second childhood,
unhindered by a mid-life crisis, a bit adventurous
bordering on the romantic, I love being along the
water and having a glass of red wine at sunset and
am looking for a younger woman.

Outside it's getting colder. I'll have to turn the heater up. But still I miss the real warmth, the warmth that starts from within. This is why I am seeking you . . . the woman who can bring me warmth.

Even if I was hanging on the cross I would be looking on the bright side of things. I am a man looking for a woman.

I know the sadness, I know the pain, leading to madness, all life in vain. I know a love that was meant, but can no longer be. Please, somebody, out there, rescue me!

Greying male pigeon is looking for solo-flying dove in order to fly together.

Come hide with me. I have an adrenaline-free bomb shelter and plenty to do. I write about peace and clowns. But what good does it do if you don't get to me before the Bomb falls. Come hide with me. In my shelter.

High priest working on a mystical and magical brotherhood is looking for a woman between 18 and 27 to be trained for the function of high priestess.

HOSTAGE. Woman, your (new) boyfriend has been taken hostage! The ransom is a loving letter from you.

Woman! You're thirty and beautiful, satisfied and married and you have two wonderful children. Still it's late Sunday afternoon, the party was tedious, the kids are complaining and it's just started to rain. You take a look around and you scare yourself. Is this what it's all about? A man of 38 has also experienced the fright of his life!

Just as a flower needs the sun to be a flower, so does a human being need love in order to be a human being. I am a man looking for a woman in order to be happy again. Yes, to be human again.

Young man without any ideas but with money is interested in meeting girls with good ideas but without money.

The next class of guys looking for gals could be described as being 'short but sweet'. Or at least to the point. These are the kind of guys who don't leave you gasping for breath. Ready? Let's go.

Fun man seeks fun woman.

Frustrated young guy who likes getting out of bed early seeks roughly the same in a woman.

Cheerful and yet melancholy man, boyish and yet fatherly, wants a woman he won't get tired of.

Man of 50 has given up the search for an 'ideal' partner. If you have a few good qualities, maybe we can agree as to the other ones.

Hi there! My name is Hank and I'm someone who enjoys life. I'm looking for a fun, hip, and more important than anything else loving girl in order to do some fantastic things together.

Man seeks woman for relationship. Photograph desired since a face tells a lot about a person. If you can't stand your face, then I can't stand you.

Man is looking for a woman because going to the movies, talking, and having breakfast in bed at the weekends are more fun with two than one.

GOOD MORNING! Did you get enough sleep? I got this crazy idea this morning when I woke up. I plan on cooking for you . . . an easy-going unattached woman between 28 to 34. If you're hungry, drop me a few lines, enclose a photo, and who knows? See you later!

NEVER AGAIN A RELATIONSHIP!!!
Although . . . well . . . maybe . . . I just don't know. I am looking once again for a fun gal to go out with, to rap to and to make love with.

Come, come ladies! I suggest we drink a beer, have a bite to eat and then see what happens next. Or do you have maybe a better idea?

Who is willing to keep me out of the Foreign Legion? I want to fit in somewhere! Balding, bearded and sad 37-year-old is looking for a woman with a similar disposition.

Man of 33 would like to prepare a fantastic meal for a cheery woman up to the age of 40 who doesn't give a damn about her waistline and knows that Fat can be beautiful. If you would like to taste my dish, then write.

Bachelor of 35 who has been to the tropics desires to return shortly. You are a woman between 25 and 35 who understands the charms exerted by the tropics on men who are free in spirit. I would like to go back with you this time so that we may enjoy the sultry tropical nights together. Interested?

Simple man seeks a simple girlfriend.

I am looking for an attractive sporty woman to jump into the snow with me. If things begin to thaw after that, we'll just have to wait and see.

A young, dashing knight seeks a fair maiden.

Is it possible to do this without a lot of bla-bla-bla? I'm a man and I'm looking for a woman. Write me and we'll take it from there.

Which dark-haired beauty dares to send me a titillating letter?

It would appear to be quite elementary, my dear Mrs Watson. You write me and we'll catch the criminal.

Do women only want 'real' men? Well that I'm not . . . simply a tall, thin anti-hero who still would like a girlfriend.

Man of 46 would like to meet the fattest woman in the world.

Prince Charming seeks a Sleeping Beauty waiting to be kissed.

Man with good job seeks well-filled deep freeze up to age 30. Purpose: marriage.

I would like to get that feeling again. Which girl would like to fall in love?

Youthful man seeks a tough-ass gal with guts. For example, a body-builder, motorcycle rider, rugby player or hard-rock girl.

A jogger who is not an absolute fanatic would like to meet a jogging girlfriend to jog twice a week.

Lovingest guy in the whole world is looking for the toughest gal (say, from a girl's reformatory) for a blooming romance and a bright future.

Fairy-tale princesses need not respond! But if you are a normal, progressive woman around 22, then I would like to meet you. I am a man of 22.

Flamethrower seeks woman with fire in her eyes.

Unattached male seeks female teddy bear to go to the sauna once a week.

Men are often after only one thing. I, a guy of 35, would also like to talk, laugh and eat out with you.

If you would like to be carried across my threshold and are light enough to do so, then we're already two points ahead. I am a man of 37 looking for a girlfriend, for now or forever.

I know how to boil water and I would like to be brought to the 'boiling point' by an active intelligent woman who would enjoy doing things together.

Is there a woman who isn't a TV-addict? Perhaps even a woman who doesn't have a TV? TV-hating man of 26 awaits your response.

Impossible kind of guy, ugly and creepy-looking, terribly egocentric and an alcoholic to boot – in short, an awful person – is looking for a girlfriend.

Some men choose to list adjectives, either to describe themselves or the 'Beauty' whom they seek.

STOP! Are you the long-legged BEAUTY up to 39 with a wardrobe ranging from jeans to tube tops, beach sandals to spiked heels, who loves French bread, snails and the south of France and who is able to view things as being relative? In short, the woman who would never respond to this kind of ad. Give me – a man of 47 – the pleasure of meeting you . . . or don't you dare?

I have more than enough women in the way of girlfriends but I am searching for the woman I could really fight for. The 'True Love'. She is soft, sweet, smart, funny, talkative, unaffected, assertive, whole, and very, very feminine.

Draw your bowstring back and shoot the following arrows off in my direction: WOMAN, 35 to 45, unattached, tennis, theatre, walking along the beach and bicycling. Not all your arrows have to hit the bull's eye and I promise to retrieve them with great pleasure and will make certain they get back to you. Please attach to one of your arrows a photo of yourself.

MADONNA is not my type. I am a man looking for an affectionate, homeloving woman in order to build towards something that will last.

He thinks that she is probably JEWISH because that's where his roots are. He has just turned 40 and their ages differ by about ten years. Their careers give the same picture, although he may be a little further: creative top position with all the hectic consequences that entails. Their interests run parallel: travel, literature, music, debates, culinary tastes. He is a bit of an introvert, she probably isn't, but both are self-assured. They both can follow the same path together so long as the eye is pleased to the same degree as the intellect. Who is this woman?

A man of 27 with ideals, fantasy, intuition, feelings, common sense, doubts, power, growing awareness and ups and downs. Sometimes without energy and without anything to say. Going through change. Emancipating. And hoping to meet you, a woman.

HELLO, WOMAN! Who am I looking for? Someone who can feel at ease and relax in the arms of another. Someone who you can trust, knows how to have fun and to whom you can say anything you want, without worrying that you might say the wrong thing. In short, I'm looking for harmony. Maybe that's expecting too much, seeing that I only have myself to give in return. I don't own a home. Or a yacht. Or even a video. I have only a few friends and I like baroque music. I am honest and have no 'past'. How about you? If you decide to write, then you're a wonderful woman.

There's someone for everyone, although . . . complicated male Aquarian, 46, bald on top, single since his birth, internationally-oriented entrepreneur, extremely busy, a non-practising Roman Catholic, socially and politically active, an aversion for ultra-right and bleeding-heart liberals, American-minded but yet anti-capitalist, a lover of Russia and its people and as such anti-Communist, an optimist to the grave and an activist. Political prisoners are the modern day heroes. I am a vegetarian, crazy about cats and believe in animal rights: I'm against hunting, vivisection and the bio-industry. I enjoy art and music as well as women and I need a female who is my equal very, very much. But please . . . no knitting types.

Falling down, getting up again and growing. Time after time. Warm man of 52 would like to share this path with a woman who understands.

Man seeks female alter ego. I am 35, not a go-getter, part-time job, would rather wear Levis than a three-piece suit, honest and vulnerable, serious and trustworthy. Sometimes sloppy, lazy or complaining but more often than not easy-going and humorous (or so they say). I enjoy modern literature (Salinger) and both classical and pop music (Glenn Gould, Pergolesi & Dire Straits) as well as TV, walking along the beach, rolling my own cigarette and drinking Bacardi (at home, naturally). I don't have any problems going it alone (well, within reason) but I don't plan on doing so the rest of my life because I know it can be better with two. The woman I am looking for is intelligent, monogamous, interested in others, has her own interests and pursuits and is someone whom I have yet to run into at parties or in the bus. She also feels like I do that she would like to have someone at her side. The expectation? No paradise on earth and yet mutual respect and inspiration for each other. A friend who won't plan my week for me. Someone who won't lay claim to me but who, every now and then, will make a wish on a star with me and/or do the dishes. In short, someone who can appreciate that another person can be special, regardless of how corny that may sound. Of course, this is a leap in the unknown for you, but since you have read this, you might as well write something back to me.

Do you happen to have a 'light' for me? Good-looking, unattached male would like to get to know a woman. Key words? None. Well, if you insist, maybe one. Winnie the Pooh.

▼▼▼▼▼▼

Loneliness and alone. Not everyone admits to this . . . but some men do!

I'm a non-conformist, not so young any more, who can handle being alone but not being lonely. I seek a jewel of a woman who isn't interested in superfluous luxuries but who is interested in music, nature and feelings.

Alone in the bar, alone in the disco and alone in bed. I am a 23-year-old male who is tired of this routine. I am choosy but am 'desperately' prepared to set aside my principles for an exciting, loving female up to age 25. Pseudo-progressives, quasi-intellectuals and those who are simply naive need not respond.

LONELY
am I without you . . . a young woman. Write to me, a man of 28.

YOUNG LADY, did your engagement end as unexpectedly as mine did? Please write to me to lighten your heart and so that we may cry it out of our systems together. A willing ear on your part will be rewarded with a broad shoulder of a 26-year-old man.

Which woman longing for love would like to meet a man of 47 whose wife has been sick for many years now in order to break through the loneliness?

My path is a varied and adventuresome one, sometimes even steep, heading on high to some very beautiful spots in this life. I am 35, male, romantic, and curious as to what is just down the road and beyond the horizon. I am also tired of being alone. The 'woman in the haystack' dances on her own two beautiful feet, is around 30, has a spontaneous laugh and a warm heart and enjoys travel, a good book and a glass of wine. Write me!

Love does not mean gazing endlessly at each other but rather is two people looking in the same direction. I have experienced that life is too short and that being together is too precious to go on like this by myself. I am a man of 32.

DREAM PRINCE is ready, willing and able to help you overcome your loneliness, bashfulness, uncertainty and feelings of inadequacy. The last three may prove to be difficult but the first will be a piece of cake.

Hello, you good-looking woman, you. If you have licked your wounds just as I have – a man of 34 – and believe in equality and tolerance, then I'd like to hear from you.

To be quite honest, I've had it with doing everything on my own. I am a young man, a bit wacky, who would like a woman to share the ups and downs. Hopefully more ups than downs.

Man of 38 is sick and tired of being lonely after four years. I am looking for a woman for a serious relationship.

Male artist has had it with eating alone and is looking for a woman who would like to cook for him, now and then.

If you are withdrawn, lonely, frigid . . . and a woman, then write me.

▼▼▼▼▼▼

Some men placing an advertisement feel it necessary to mention the ad itself, as if to acknowledge that the approach is, well, a trifle unusual.

If I were to meet you accidentally, then I am certain I would approach you. However, that 'accident' would be a long time coming in this fast life of ours we live in. Therefore, I must resort to this. I am a man of 34 who has still to run across you in my own surroundings. But I know you must be out there – somewhere – and without this ad I would probably not reach you. Who knows what the future may hold?

I have yet to come across you spontaneously so I'm going to try this way. I'm a man of 30, own my own business and am looking for a gal not older than 25 who can get by without using make-up.

A complete, total woman between the ages 47 and 52. This is who I want. You can't force things in life. Still I'm going to try this. John.

It's a pretty crazy idea to sit down and make an ad for yourself. Still, here goes: I'm a man of 35 who would like to walk again through the city with his arms around a woman. Love and freedom don't necessarily go together, but I'm beginning to understand how that might be possible. I get along with kids okay and, other than that, what more would you like to know? Send your questions to . . .

This is probably the most effective and fastest way to get to you. I am a man of 32 seeking a loving woman who enjoys an active love life.

Maybe this isn't the ideal way of doing it . . . but I'm going to try, anyway. Young man seeks ideal woman for serious relation.

To place an ad like this calls for daring and to respond to such an ad demands courage, because everyone knows this is a leap into the unknown. For me to sell myself as an attractive young man makes no sense since everyone looks at things differently. The first meeting usually says it all. Why not take a chance just as I have. Who knows what might happen?

▼▼▼▼▼▼

Some would argue you are who you are in your leisure time. Others would argue you are who you are from 9 to 5. The latter would be drawn to the next class of ads, all pointing to a man's profession.

Veterinarian still seeking single litter mate with a kitten's charming playfulness, a puppy's unqualified love, this man's matchless best friend. Honesty, romance important; pedigree not. Pets optional.

Attorney, 53, Hip Hebrew Hedonist, marriagephobic. Smoker, drinker and former boxer. Seeks adventurous, brainy broad for intimate friendship.

Electrical engineer, back two years after a six-year stint in the tropics, seeks a hip woman who has taken a good look around and knows what she wants.

I am a 38-year-old tax consultant with my own practice. I am known by people who know me as a friendly and even spontaneous person. Due to any number of reasons, most notably a prolonged study, my opportunities to meet a woman have been rather limited. Fortunately, things have changed for the better. That's why I'm looking for a girlfriend. Unmarried, divorced, with or without child(ren). Someone you can talk to, has a sense of humour and is well-developed as a person. Between the ages of 25 and 40. I am not out for sex . . . but I am a great fan of popular music.

Artistic painter seeks loving Rubenesque woman.

Sensitive man of 46 with management function is looking for a woman in order to build up together a balanced relationship and to go walking together in the sun and the rain.

To Tathinou in 1987. Painter, sailor, storyteller and construction worker seeks woman who would like to go sailing, to work . . . and to live.

Doctor who enjoys Mozart, travel and warmth, would like to meet a good-looking gal around the age of 30.

Dentist would like to meet woman for oral examination.

Which sensitive young woman would like to have contact with a 29-year-old male prisoner who is sitting out a lengthy prison term? I need a woman who can experience a relation as being meaningful without there being much of a perspective for the future. If desired, the first contact can be arranged through my religious advisor.

I promise you no Rose Garden. Businessman of 45 with his own company and a £100,000 mortgage seeks a stable, trustworthy WOMAN.

Self-supporting research engineer, well-off, no problems, has paid off on a house that is too big and is seeking an attractive woman who likes animals.

Sailor, 48, unattached, seeks woman up to 45 for shore leaves.

Airline mechanic in good condition, resembles a teddy bear, owns nice house and loves to have fun, seeks younger, fun-loving woman who treasures laughing, talking, travelling and outdoor activities.

Grey-haired, beat-up police sergeant, divorced, uncouth, has to work nights and can't dance. Send your letter before demand skyrockets and your competition gets too tough.

Writer seeks uncommon denominator for a jazz lunch, bike trip to China, tropic expedition, sunrise horseride, tête à tête dual, avec coeur inclination.

French businessman and sportsman, 42, divorced, romantic, adventurous, trilingual, travels between French castle and beachside Bahamas house, seeks company in the form of an attractive and compatible lady.

SPECIAL OFFER – THIS WEEK ONLY. Farmer, 39, seeks woman who is willing to help out around the farm (although that really isn't necessary). If this appeals to you and you don't suffer from romantic notions about farm life, I'd like to hear from you.

Are you crazy about clouds, wind and water? Gardening? And animals? Then where are you? I'm a fisherman, getting on in his thirties, who would like to share his hut with you, an attractive woman. Come on, let's hear something from you, have a chat around the fireside with a glass of wine. That won't obligate you in the least.

Astronomer, 30, introvert, not 'always there' by nature but still spontaneous at times, would like to meet a young woman.

Illustrator, 36, has had it with all that modern stuff and would like to have a good old-fashioned relationship within which each partner remains strong and so forth and so on. I'm looking for a good-looking gal with ballet legs and a skirt.

Author seeks female reader/writer. Purpose: long-lasting, stimulating friendship.

Violinist would like to meet female pianist.

Former mineworker, 31, seeks a country girl for some folk music.

Sculptor seeks woman with inspirational figure. Purpose: to make something beautiful together.

▼▼▼▼▼▼

Some men are looking to do what others claim is impossible: to mix 'business' with pleasure.

I am a man of 32 leaving for Portugal to buy a farm. But I'd rather not do that by myself. Which woman craves adventure?

Physical therapist seeks energetic, dynamic girlfriend from the alternative sector (massage, healing) in order to set up 'SOMETHING' together.

Man seeks woman to go to Canary Islands to live and work together.

Attractive young man of 27 seeks female life partner for a unique camp ground and farm in the south of France. I love animals, archery & Supertramp

Sometimes money – or the lack of it – is important. Or unimportant.

Wealthy-beyond-belief individual, 52, seeks unattached and good-looking woman for travel up to the age of 40.

Sensitive, loving man seeks understanding, sensitive and very wealthy woman up to the age of 55.

Which gal would like to have an open but extremely pleasurable relationship with a guy of 37 who enjoys going out and making out. There is no lack of money to do all the things you always wanted to do. And with TWO it can be a lot more fun!

Wealthy gentleman, 46, seeks young girl as au-pair help or for vacation trips.

Attractive man of 30 interested in meeting a woman from good background for serious relation. Most important is that she be willing to support him.

If one doesn't have money, there's always music. And a shared inferest in listening to . . . classic. Or pop. Or jazz or rock.

Peace-loving man would like to meet peaceful woman. Passwords: Music, including, but not limited to . . . T. Waits, Ry Cooder, G. Isaacs, J. Martyn, Springsteen, Costello, Morrison, J. Hiatt, K. Coyne, Clash, U2, E and the B, Little Feat, African music, soul music and everything yet to come.

Which music-loving woman will write me, a music-loving man of 45?

'The blues ain't nothin' but a good man feelin' bad,' said BB King. Which young woman is ready to get it on with a blues fanatic, male, 33, during a 12-hour blues festival next weekend?

I love music: The Fixx and Billy Idol. I love to look like a Punk and to be Punk and to be seen with Punk. I also like to work out with my body. I work at a job the last three years, but it doesn't matter to me if someone works . . . or doesn't. I like tempo and pace. I am both tough and soft. I am a man. I want a girlfriend.

Young man, Zappa crazy, likes fixing up old houses (thus a very busy life), would like to meet a young woman.

SULTAN OF SWING (male, 31) seeks a 'sister in arms' for the 'walk of life'. Getting along with each other is more important than key words so long as your wanderlust extends further than Benidorm.

Motorcycle prince desires motorcycle princess with a phobia for cars and a soft spot for New Wave music.

Dylan, Bach, erotica and submission. Man seeks woman to undergo music, pleasure and beauty under his experienced tutelage.

A nightingale cannot sing in a cage! Man seeks woman who would like to sing together without caging one another.

I would like to see you laughing in 'the purple rain'. PRINCE seeks a fantasy princess to fall in love with and to be super happy.

Then there are those who simply want a serious, long-lasting relationship. Perhaps more old-fashioned than romantic, their collective message is loud and clear.

It may not be enough, but it could make a difference to our future if you find yourself in the following words: respect, honesty, faithfulness. If you feel like getting something out of life with a guy in his early fifties, if you are unattached, a woman and not yet 40, and if you look at life with a grin and a clear conscience, then grab this chance to be with me. Which woman out there desires to join in with me in adding a new dimension to the word 'relation'?

Man with disability compensation is seeking a young woman in order to overcome our mutual inhibitions, to enjoy each other, to discover and complement one another and to grow towards a cosmic state of being filled with life-energizing love and meaningful assistance.

Without love there is a lot you cannot accomplish by yourself in this world. I tend to realize this more and more. In spite of a hell of a good job I miss a lot of what could make my daily existence truly great. The placer of this dead serious ad is a man of 36. I am looking for a woman who, just like me, longs for a relation within which spiritual and sexual contact of a lasting and satisfying nature can only be expected.

Kind of ugly and rather corpulent middle-aged man, unmarried, well-off but not particularly intelligent, is looking for a pretty, chubby woman in order to become seriously happy.

Self-sufficient man seeks female alter ego to share the daily worries but also to have some fun, a few laughs, to cuddle and kiss, to breathe the fresh air outside and to watch TV, too. And someone who will leave me alone when I simply don't want to do anything.

I am a loving, attractive man of 30 who desires the same in a woman in order to experience the most wonderful thing that there is . . . to love and be loved.

Single man seeks single woman who would not mind living with a somewhat older guy in an honest fashion on a farm. Preferably someone with a working-class/blue-collar background.

Man, 37, single, warm and tender, seeks single woman for a passionate and loving relationship based on mutual respect for each other. It would be wonderful to rub each others' bodies and excite one another. Do you also like to fall asleep – naked – in someone else's arms? I long for your soft skin and breasts. I am not an egoist, but if things 'click' I'm sure I could be really good for you.

Not all women need reply to this ad. Only those who think they are looking for friendship but secretly hope to find love. I am a man.

They tell me I have beautiful brown eyes. The rest of me also looks pretty good – I hope (gulp!). Man of 25 with extremely high caress and cuddle factor (8½ on a scale of 10) seeks a girlfriend up to 30 for something lasting and beautiful.

Divorced man of 49 seeks new life partner with an interest and a vision which is broader than her front doorstep.

I don't have gold and I don't have money. I don't believe in fairy tales and I don't really have much of a career. What I do have though is the following: spontaneity; a character which you can trust and build on; and a belief that life is worthwhile, the more so if you are 'together'. If you feel the same way, that being 'alone' is not really your style, then maybe it's time we got to know each other.

Once a guy gets that 'serious', he's not too far away from wanting a child. Kids. Maybe even a family. And some men come right out and ask for it.

I am a man of 33 and would like to have a child. I am looking for a woman who would like to be the mother, but doesn't want to be completely responsible for his care and upbringing.

Indonesian man is looking on the basis of reincarnation for a life partner in order to start a family.

I am a friendly, sensitive man and seek a spontaneous honest woman who doesn't believe in conforming to foreordained roles. Children are welcome.

Artistic male seeks single MOTHER up to 40 for a fine future.

Which Rubenesque woman would like a monogamous relation without taboos, to be able to laugh, to cry, to share, to make love and to long for a family life?

Up-and-coming father seeks up-and-coming mother.

TO BE A FATHER is my fondest desire. At the age of 40 I am still young enough to make this dream come true. Before I was often overseas due to my work. At the time I thought I could adopt a child in the Third World, but as a bachelor that proved to be impossible. That is why I am doing this now. I would gladly take on the full or partial responsibility for one or two kids from the age of 2 years on.

Of course, a man may already be well on his way to a family and need only a woman to complete the circle.

Young man, 33, is looking for a girlfriend. Young man, 9, would like to have a mother again. Is there a chance? We sure hope so!

I am a boy of 4 with a pappa of 43. We are both looking for more sunshine and happiness. We are also looking for a woman, with or without child(ren). We live in a beautiful house all our own and my Dad has a nice income. In spite of this very business-like ad I would much rather have a letter from you. So go on and write!

Brother and sister, 8 and 5 years old respectively, are looking for a mother to take care of us and our father aged 36.

When you have kids, pets can't be too far behind. This trip would not be complete without an excursion into the land of 'man's best friend'. (Do I hear someone miaowing in the background?)

LOVE is the only freedom in a programmed world. Male poet (28), with a canine who occasionally 'poops' on the doorstep and who believes in plastic as well as roses, seeks artistic woman in order to discover what previously simply did not exist!

I am a 31-year-old bachelor who most people think is a pretty nice guy. I am looking for an exciting, vivacious woman and am caught up with my business. The only leisure activity I enjoy is taking my dog for a walk in the forest. Other than that I am a bit of a homebody and for this reason rather boring to most people. If you see something worthwhile in me, then please send me a letter.

Man of 33 seeks a nice woman to cook for, to eat with, to walk the dog with, to go to the movies with and to have a beer. And, after a while maybe to live with. Bitches, hysterical types and pushy feminists need not respond.

Man seeks lady friend. Must not like cats.

If you are a woman from 30 onwards who has had her fill of loose relations then maybe you might want to write me, a man of 38. I live together with my daughter and four cats. By the way, I am no Prince Charming on a white horse and there is plenty wrong with me. But if you happen to be in my neighbourhood and should you be interested, give me a ring.

A cat usually goes his own way but does need affection every now and then. That's why a manly 30-year-old CAT is looking for a girlfriend. For a little affection. Every now and then.

Leaving man's 'best friend' aside for the moment, something else is also near and dear to every man. His holidays and his vacation. Isn't it natural he would wish to share these with someone?

Xmas is approaching rapidly. Man, 52, birthday on Xmas, is looking for a suitable female companion to celebrate both the Christmas and the New Years. We have three months to get to know each other.

Is there a woman out there who would like to accompany me on vacation, for free, to a warm and sunny land?

I am a businessman who will be sailing away very shortly for warmer climes and I intend to stay away until this awful winter has passed. I'm looking for a fellow sailor. She should be young, romantic and a bit crazy in a nice sort of way. Do you still exist?

Man seeks woman for coming holidays and, if it 'clicks', for even cozier days well into the New Year.

I am tired of going off on adventures by myself and seek an adventuresome woman to accompany me. Where to? To the Sahel, the Sahara or the Sudan. When? Tomorrow or the next day.

Have you ever been to Istanbul or Budapest or perhaps Prague? And still there is so much more to see. For you, for me; for you and me together. I am a man who likes art, literature, music and an arm around me. You are a woman who fits into that picture. Purpose: a fine, lasting relation.

Man of 34 seeks well-balanced woman for journey through China. I hope at the same time to meet a travel companion for the rest of my life.

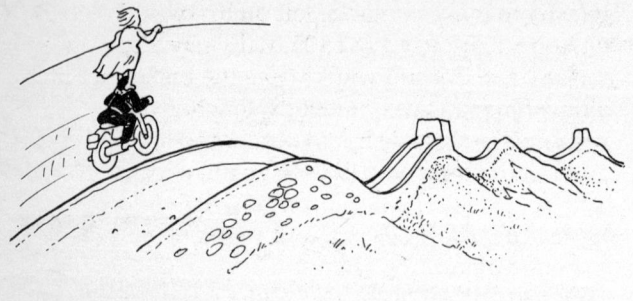

▼▼▼▼▼▼

If that wasn't enough – all those men, all looking for women – some men don't even have to lift a finger. That's right. Others do it for them.

I am placing this ad on behalf of my good friend. John is still a bachelor, is shy around women but would like to meet a nice woman between 30 and 40. John has his own business, a car, a boat and a second house in Switzerland. He is pleasant to be with and kind of quiet. Come on, Girls, let's hear something from you. Write . . . and John will do the rest.

We are looking for a woman for our neighbour, George. Someone who is energetic, spunky and who might be able to bring a little extra something into his life.

I am looking for a girlfriend for my brother who is 46. She should be gentle, be well-educated and have an interest for natural foods. Preferably childless.

I am looking for a girlfriend for my buddy at the pub. Personality more important than looks.

We are looking on behalf of our son who is 35 and too shy to make contact if left on his own. We seek an honest girl, aged 28 to 35, who may also be a bit too shy and doesn't want to live the rest of her life alone. Our son is a homebody so whoever responds to this ad should be a home-loving type and not the type who likes to go out a lot.

Last but not the least are the 'LONG' ads. The lengthy ones. The ads which sometimes run a whole column. Some people say you can measure a man by the length of his ad. If anyone knows for sure, she isn't saying.

As autumn descends and the leaves begin to blow off the trees outside, it's time to draw up the balance sheet and take a break. A sensitive man of 37 does not want to give up the hope that he will meet his female alter ego and one day be able to hold her close to him without suffocating each other. He is in no way macho, but is leftist and 'emancipated' towards women. He is against charlatans and Pharisees and is in favour of integrity, caring and being each other's sounding board. He is independent and has a creative function and his own house. Many books and records. He enjoys contrasts and contradictions. Wild evenings and quiet moments. From Bach to Big Band. Everything from backpack vacations to lying along the beach and doing nothing at all. He eats little meat, a bit more fish and hasn't smoked in years. He believes in people and looks more to their actions and deeds than their words. Which woman recognizes herself in the foregoing passages? Someone about the same age who knows how to live, how to dress and is good with languages. And who also doesn't mind acting a little crazy at times. She should write an extended letter in which a part of herself comes to the surface. Who knows . . . perhaps New Year's Eve will be spent together, after all!

I would love to meet the charming, spiritually strong woman who doesn't deny the pain in her past but enjoys unshakeable faith in the future. A woman from a good background who is tender and sympathetic and yet is dynamic in her actions and ways. I am 50 and own an export company. My name is Jack and I smoke a pipe. I like most of all to spend my free time chatting, working in the garden, going out, playing bridge, reading, swimming, practising a positive form of nudism/ naturalism. I am extremely monogamous and find the accidental touching and connecting with each other the crowning touch of life itself. Who is the ideal woman? She has an affinity for business, is representative, has diverse interests and knows many things, has a sense of humour and is considerate, appreciates the attention given to her and has the wisdom which comes from leading a full life, is thin and trim, around 40 and probably has black hair. I am a Gemini/Virgin and your star sign is preferably Aries/Libra/Aquarius. I would like to hear from you, together with a snapshot.

CHAPTER 3 ▬▬▬

If men have it rough, then women have it tough. Being a woman in to-day's world is no picnic. In the good old days, the would-be huntress need only let fall a handkerchief in the proximity of a man, or 'accidentally' show a little ankle. Those tactics would hardly prove effective in to-day's world of both bottomless and topless beaches. Quite often, the searching woman must find her solace in the personal columns, just as her male counterpart.

What's remarkable is that although women are often accused of being romantic, in the world of personals the opposite appears to be the case. Women are realists and leave the fan-tasizing to their dreamy-eyed mascu-line counterparts. Women have no delusions about men; having lived with them all their lives, they have learned to settle for less.

Who knows, if Eve had been the first to be created, she might have been content with the way things were. She would have never started writing on a papyrus leaf . . . and there wouldn't have been any men at all.

WOMAN SEEKS MAN

If men can be philosophical, poetic and simply 'cute', so can women, as the following personals give evidence to.

I believe
I believe in (nearly) everything
I am busy
I have it good
I have two kids
I am 45 and a woman
I like to laugh and a lot
I live in the north
I don't want to change any of this
But maybe a nice friend can make this even better
I have spoken
Now for you.

Mouth-watering and sparkling 'femme' du champagne dating from 1955 is looking for a warm crystal bottom in order to be brought to the right temperature. An unattached, intelligent and colourful man is desired by an attractive, intelligent lady to see if they will 'clink' together.

The summer has passed and in spite of the rain I have amused myself. With a partner on the same wavelength, the winter months are bound to get even better. I am a good-looking woman with a flair for life and in no way dependent but also find it wonderful to be able to please a man in every single way. If you meet enough women in business and socially but still not the one about whom you could say 'she has "it" for me' then by all means, write me.

Blond guy, I saw you first at the flower market. In an alleyway, where I had never been before, I touched you. Afterwards, we exchanged a few words and nothing more. I want to see you again, to talk to you a little longer this time. And to touch you!

I'm a happy woman in her forties and I ask you, do you want to be the other half of my 'BEING'? Are you well-balanced, full of life, spiritually together and sensitive, too? Do you have a free spirit? If so, I desire you as an adult human being, a man and a comrade, for now and always and, yes, forever.

When I jump on my bike and cycle into the city and see all those big, gorgeous hunks of manhood, then I think back to how wonderful it is to make love. If you were to ask me how I'm doing, I'd say that everything's just fine. But still, when I sing a tune, I'm not really able to put my whole heart and soul into it. I was lucky, once. If I don't watch out, I'm sure I'll be lucky again. I'm a widow who's spent a part of her life in South America and I am looking for an unattached man/friend/father who is not set in his ways and has a thousand and one plans.

WANTED!

A long and lanky guy who would like to make history – and go into history – with an artistic gal of 40.

If you
Would like to do more things together
Are a man
Have a sense of humour
Like Bach
And children
Are politically to the left
Like to go camping
Enjoy living outside
Give off warmth
Are a feeling person
Live with your body
And love art
Then there are a number of points of common interest. I am a woman of 37, have a creative job, and am full of plans.

He who loves life, who does not look down on love and who becomes lost in rapture while listening to music of all kinds but would prefer experiencing this together with a woman . . . HE will write ME!

Hello, dear one. So long as I miss you and long for you as a woman, so long as I miss your warmth within which I can flower and blossom and give more sunny tenderness to the meaning of life every single day, so long as . . . After the hurricane, let's have a little rest, you know what I mean?

Energetic VENUS in Aries seeks her MARS in Aquarius who can deal with her moon in Cancer.

Playful female mouse seeks shameless male louse.

I am bursting with sexual energy but am unable to share this with my partner. Are you the self-confident man who is looking for that rare source of inspiration who will bring you closer to yourself and with whom you can climb to unheard of heights before finally letting go? If you are, then this woman overcome with fiery passion is looking to hear from you.

Woman with two napkin holders is looking for a loving man with a white napkin.

I am looking for a male friend who doesn't have a suit, who views a tent as being a hotel, who likes daffodils and strays from the trodden paths, who enjoys a sandwich on wholewheat bread and knows what empathy means, who knows how to make life a party and is between 45 and 55.

The journey (in)to myself (woman, 36) begins NOW, departing from the ME to the TOGETHER.

I am seeking a mirror for my soul, a sounding board for my voice and a conductor for my warmth. Woman, 40.

Men can place ads that are 'short and sweet', but women can be 'shorter' and even 'sweeter'.

If you should suffer from a 'sweet' tooth, you may wish to sink your teeth into these.

Mischievous girl of 24 is searching for an appealing masculine apparition of loveliness up to age 30 whose brain cells are not all on non-active, who enjoys red wine and who is fun to be with. Are you out there, handsome?

Normal woman seeks normal relation with normal man.

'Hot but shy' woman is looking for a tender, strong, male human being.

Just back from Africa, I long for warmth. I am looking for a rough and tough boyfriend, around 30. Easy-going and not a coward, I am a woman.

Woman seeks light-footed man with depth in order to have some fun.

FANTASY OR REALITY. Can I find the unbridled fervour of a brother and the years of experience of a father in one man?

Woman with beard seeks man.

An intriguing hello from a free man who lives in harmony with himself and has an interest for the supernatural could add an extra dimension to the birthday of this attractive, spiritual woman of 40.

Chubby mother of 39 seeks a well-built man.

A single lady with a first-class education is looking for a medical doctor. An African or American Negro would do just fine.

Charming lady seeks well-bred gentleman from good background in order to laugh and to cry and to enjoy the finer things in life, together.

Woman bicyclist, 42, seeks a man with both a body and a soul for anything and everything.

Uggh! All the good-looking guys have already been taken. Yes, they're married! Uggh! Is there a single guy out there around 42 who would like to have some fun with a woman around the same age going to concerts, films, theatre and so on. Eating out, travel, skiing. Good music accompanied by a glass of wine and a cigarette or cigar. Yes, write me!

Ha Ha. Gal seeks guy as mate. Please, not married or living with somebody.

Woman, 32, Libra, feminist, seeks androgynous man for a fruitful relationship. Neurotics, pseudo-intellectuals and mental misfits need not respond.

Endless love-making, friendship . . . but no commitments. Woman, 30, seeks man between 28 and 38. Money doesn't count; you do!

Woman of 30 misses action-packed relation and a child. Man wanted!!!

Woman, 23, seeks a combination teddy bear and
Wild West cowboy who is interested in raising his
consciousness and believes in meditation. I don't
expect you to make me happy, only that we have
some fun together.

Woman, 30, seeks her True Love. Which scaredy-
cat dares to answer?

Attractive woman with a good set of brains would
like a different set of masculine hands on occasion.

Okay! All you single guys out there who are hiding
in your rabbit holes . . . COME ON OUT! I'm a
modern gal of 28.

I've got a crush on my dentist. Wouldn't you
know, he's married. Which guy around 50 will
help me change my mind?

I would love to meet the guy who believes in
reincarnation, who is a sharp thinker, respects
himself and is good to me. Age, hobbies and
occupation are unimportant. I'm a woman of 40.

Is there a guy out there between 35 and 45 who
looks like Brian Ferry and has had it with hanging
out in singles bars? I'm a widow of 40.

Woman with energy seeks aristocrat who makes
life as he lives it.

Woman, 40, seeks CAMEL-FILTER man who
doesn't smoke.

Who, oh who, appreciates and understands that everything is relative and temporary and is willing to share that notion with me. I am a woman of 46 with experiences which continually confirm what I firmly believe.

Woman seeks man who likes animals and nature.

You know the type of woman, the type who by the age of 40 has everything going her way: a good job, active social life, lots of friends, cats and so forth. Successful, it's called. Well, that woman is now looking for the guy for whom none of that makes a difference.

I'm a woman who would like to spend a weekend with the first guy who comes up with the craziest – wildest – lovingest suggestion.

Are all the reliable men taken or is there still one walking around loose out there? Woman of 31 is dying of curiosity.

I've been in love, engaged and married before. Now I'm ready to do it all over again. Woman of 40 with a mixed bag of personal idiosyncracies and 'character' traits, seeks her male alter ego who also happens to be 'free'.

Woman would like to meet spiritual man to be sent out to the Third World.

I am looking for a male connoisseur for my new Italian recipe. A man of around 40 who can enjoy eating and living life together.

Woman, 46, with job, car, flat and unwilling to radically change present way of living hopes to meet a guy for an extra dimension without obligations.

Which angry young man would like to go with an intelligent and sensitive woman to an Afro-Latin music evening?

I am a well-travelled woman, age 36. Sometimes I dream about a future containing a man and kids in a faraway tropical land. But I also have both feet firmly planted on the ground. Interested?

▼▼▼▼▼▼

Some women also choose to use strings of adjectives, either to describe their 'Beauty' or the 'Beast' they hope to catch.

Before I decide to simply run off and join a cloister, a few personal details: I'm a woman, 29, who is looking for a man not fixated on conformity and who is religious and able to deal with his feelings. I work in education and enjoy theatre, cabaret, film, music, reading, strolling, cycling, travel and most recently sailing.

I am a woman in her late thirties who has only recently 'blossomed'. Sometimes I'm emancipated, sometimes I'm not. Sometimes I'm intellectual and sometimes not in the least. I seek a tender friend with a set of brains and a feel for the erotic. A man who has learned from life that things can be other than how they seem at first.

Free – seabird – sea – movement – sun – intense – warmth – life – body – tender – giving – surrender – vulnerable – together – home – hands – doing – walking – cycling – strolling – nature – music – New Age consciousness. Which single man would like to 'team up' with this woman?

I am a woman full of contradictions: difficult – loving – cheerful – bitchy – sloppy – realistic – vegetarian – and (still) a smoker. I am not pretty, charming or particularly intelligent. I am shy, uncertain and a daydreamer. I seek a male friend without a car, status or money in order to love him.

Woman seeks man to have fun. Key words: football, cuddling, reading and pussycats.

WANTED: friendly, thin male sailor up to 40 years. OFFERED: woman, 34, self-supporting, uncertain, sense of humour, friendly, a bit cynical. UNWANTED: fat, bearded, goat socks and formal ties. RESULT?

Woman, 40, seeks male friend for cycling, eating, sleeping, talking, laughing, going to the show, vacations in Hungary and staying young.

I am looking for a mate, an adult man, who isn't looking for his mother, isn't afraid of a strong woman and who has the courage to be loving. I am a woman of 37, creative, warm and open.

I'm a woman who is looking for a guy. Not a macho but not a softie, either. A warm, open man with guts and a lust for life who has a sense of humour and is strong enough to take me on.

Does this guy really exist? A combination of intelligence, forthrightness, humorous, attractive, without financial or alcohol problems, between 38 and 48 who would desire a woman around 39, divorced nearly three years, with a good job, music- and sport-minded and reasonably independent.

BIRTHDAY GIFT? Where the hell is that relationship with a thin, good-looking guy around 40. I'm a woman (41) who doesn't have anything against smoking, drinking, or doing a little soft drugs but I don't like conservative balls. Gentlemen, paper and pen are not your enemies.

Woman of 29 enjoys good conversation, good books and good music and would like to meet an understanding, intelligent guy between 25 and 40 who enjoys both literal and figurative games.

Attractive woman of 43, overflowing with life, desires a man to love her who is powerful enough to be weak when necessary, is smart enough to know when to play stupid, who has a sense of humour and doesn't run away from his problems, who also doesn't really know what a new relation might mean but is ready, willing and able to take a chance and find out.

Do you have the feeling that in spite of all your experience you are still an absolute beginner when it comes to making love? Are you wiser but hardly happier? Do you still retain a bit of optimism and daring? Then write me, you wonderful, good-looking, undoubtedly intelligent and caring single man of between 40 and 50. I am a woman of 40 who is self-sufficient and affectionate, spontaneous and unconventional, not a beauty but thin and most assuredly pleasant to be with.

Woman, 30, serious, easy-going, sensitive, home-loving, doesn't smoke and so on and so on is looking for a man for a serious relation. Do you sail? Have you ever been to Scandinavia – I haven't, Ha Ha! I love to sail anything that makes life easier and maybe you!

▼▼▼▼▼▼

Alone, alone. At home and on the phone. Alone, alone. Women on their own. And wanting to change . . . alone.

Woman of 30 is tired of being all alone. I would like to meet a man to work towards building a fine future.

When I come home at night I would like, once again, to feel two arms wrap their way around me. A kiss on the neck. And then a glass of wine. Shared. Together. I am 31, working in health care, and seek a loving mate. Someone for whom I can mean something and he for me.

I am like I am, what can I do? I've got a heart like everyone else. I hate to be alone and yet am afraid of losing my freedom. What to do? Everyone wants someone but some just don't know how. Everyone goes his own way but who knows where? Which man will extend to me a hand? P.S. Even a simple friendship can enrich your life.

I find it deplorable to only live for myself and my two cats without being able to share my deeper feelings with someone else. That's why someone like me – a woman of 31 – is looking for a sympathetic male who also needs friendship within an honest, warm and monogamous relationship.

Woman, 28, expressive, spontaneous, bashful, sensitive, sweet but not easy, has everything from friendships to a good job. But after two years of living alone, I long for a man in order to build something lasting within which we can be messy together and still go our own way. Ever so often I come across an intrusive look somewhere – on the street, on my bike, in a cafe – but to speak to someone just like that just doesn't happen very often. Are you honourable, tender, passionate and not focussed on materialistic things? Then yes, please, write to me . . .

Eating, sleeping and going out by myself is okay
. . . but not all the time. Woman of 39 is looking for
an emancipated man who would like to have fun.

I AM DEFINITELY NOT A WALLFLOWER. But
due to a failed relationship, I've been alone for a
while. I have many friends and hobbies. I seek a
friend who can give to me what is now missing:
warmth, understanding and interest in each
others' interest. I am 26 and thinking of a man up
to the age of 35 who is also not a wallflower. If you
can feel what I mean, then write.

I miss the natural intimacy which comes with
being with a man. I am a 35-year-old woman who
likes her (girl)friends, a sense of humour and being
active. On the other hand, there are some things I
dislike, such as superficiality and the fact that my
taking this first step is a bit too much for me. Will
you write me?

Woman is tired of her 'independence' and is
therefore on the look out for a man. Children are
gladly welcome.

Being alone is wonderful but it isn't everything.
Woman, 51, seeks single male in order to laugh
together, cry together and to enjoy life together.

I've done as much as I could and can on my own.
Now it's time to go on further with a man of
around 37. I am a woman of 36.

Cats aren't everything, believe it or not! I'm
looking for some human kind of cuddling. I'm a
woman, 27, and I seek a man, up to 35.

Playing all by yourself is not fun! Woman, 36, seeks friend, comrade, lover. Who would like to play with me?

▼▼▼▼▼▼

Women are not so inclined to list their profession, whether or not it be the 'oldest'. Quite often, only an indication is given: professional, in education, in medicine, though others will come right out and say it.

Sexy professional woman who does not want to constantly have to prove it desires self-assured man not on ego trip. Miami Vice stars need not reply.

I am a 38-year-old female writer and painter who is beyond all cynicism. I am looking for unattached friends between 25 and 75 who are as intelligent as they are intuitive so that we might do things we can enjoy.

Woman landscaper, 39, is looking for a man with a green thumb.

I am more than simply a spunky, sensitive woman of 40 with a rich inner life and a young outward life as well as an engaging position as a psychotherapist. My heart beats for people, art and beauty. In my own life there's plenty of room for a loyal, realistic kind of guy with fantasy who would like to fall head over heels for someone. Man, have I got your attention yet, or not?

Businesswoman, 40, seeks extremely handsome single man approaching 50 who is well travelled and witty.

Do you suffer from the arrogance which comes from thinking that you are too good for this page? No matter what you may think about these personals, it's hard to tell on the street or in a bar what you may be getting yourself into, either. Female sculptor of 42 seeks a mate for bread and wine and a little fun.

Which man up to the age of 30 would like to accompany me – a nurse, age 23 – to my parents' silver marriage jubilee. What happens after that we can decide then.

I am a lonely painter. I live in a box of paints. Female painter, emotional, warm, seeks friendship and support from a masculine male for through thick and thin. Someone who isn't boring, conservative or neither here nor there. After that, we'll see what happens. Preferably another artist.

Former feminist seeks male friend who is stinking rich.

Many women, undoubtedly the majority, are looking for a serious even permanent relationship. Marriage, kids, ' . . . until death do us part'. Traditional values expressed by not always so traditional gals and girls.

I am an intelligent woman of 28 who would like to get married and have a family now that I have achieved everything I could hope for in the way of a career. Would you like a gal who waits for you at home? Are you financially secure and good towards women and children? Would you like to do everything *together*? Minimum requirements: six feet tall, no children, a sense of style and you should go to work in a suit. If you satisfy the minimum requirements and are interested, drop me a line.

How can I begin to say this in just a few sentences? By letter it's easier. In any event, I'm a woman, 32, and would like to meet a loving man. Words which mean something to me: belief, openness, faithfulness (marriage?) and working, sharing and caring for each other. If you write, you'll get an answer. I'm curious.

Only a man who aspires to be a partner and a father can stop me from entering a cloister. I am a woman who aspires to being a partner and mother.

Because of my desire to have a relation and children keeps resurfacing, this ad. I am a woman, 33, friendly, attentive, serious and critical. I have a good job and a nice home. If you are a man who loves other people, then write me.

A life lived intensely gives meaning to your very being as a person. To experience this with friends is extremely worthwhile. I would like to try and add an additional dimension to even this. This may be possible when you, a man, react to this ad. I am a woman, almost thirty & religious.

Woman would like to reap what she has sowed after 39 years. I am looking for a strong, emotionally ripe man to live together and to build a family.

Positive-oriented female yoga teacher with many-sided interests would like to find a life partner.

I am looking for a man who will buy me a big house with a gigantic garden and a high fence covered with signs saying – No Trespassing – so I can sit all day painting and playing the cello and then making a delicious meal when he comes home so we can sit down and eat together and talk and laugh and finally fall asleep in each others' arms every night for always and always.

A letter to a loving, single man between 36 and 50 who still can get amazed at things on occasion. Someone who is a bit crazy, a bit naive and can get passionate about something. I am a single woman, 36, who looks perfectly normal from the outside but is sometimes crazy on the inside, strong but weak, who believes in kids and having them, and enjoys my own place, my friends, plants and music. In short . . . everything that is alive and living. I know what it is like to live alone or together and this last is what I want the most! I'm really curious who you might be.

Woman seeks a man who is real, who can be emotional and isn't afraid to show it, but most of all someone who is honest and just, loves kids and has more to talk about than simply his work and the weather.

▼▼▼▼▼▼

Some women who have been 'serious' once are looking to get 'serious' again. Most notably those with one or two or even more kids. In fact, this is one area in which women's ads outnumber their male counterparts.

The path of life is filled with many pit holes and deep valleys surrounded by incredible beauty. But to walk this path alone is not easy; you miss two strong arms to hold you when you threaten to slip over the edge. Which serious man up to 40 would like to be a guide for a woman of 33 with two children?

As a result of a phobia my social contacts are few and far between. Because of this my self-assured and intelligent toddler is missing out on the company of family and friends. I am looking for a man who is willing to fill the gap by joining forces with us.

After three years of living and working self-sufficiently, I would like to find a man in order – once again – to start a family after a disappointing but nevertheless rewarding experience in the past. I am a 39-year-old woman with two kids and active with bio-energy, vegetarianism and sailing.

Woman with 3½-year-old child, not completely recovered from previous relation, would like to meet a man between 35–40 for an honest relation.

Have you been successful in your career and know how to see things in their proper perspective? Do you sometimes have deep emotions? Are you satisfied with yourself, do you live a creative life and are you faithful? If so, then I would like to meet you because you are the man who fits in with me: woman, 38, imaginative, full-time position, two children.

Woman of 32 with three kids seeks unattached male up to age 45 for a relation without end.

I can't keep eating myself up over a bum relationship. I'm a woman of 30 with a son of 2 who would like to meet a man who is ready to go all the way.

I am looking for a regular sort of guy in order to – DON'T GET SHOCKED NOW! – love him for the rest of my life.

Woman of 41 would like to meet a man who doesn't think three kids are a little too much. If you have a child, that's okay, too!

I'll tell you my name later. You'll have to find out for yourself who I really am. But now for a few 'details': woman, 25, spontaneous, divorced and 'in possession of' two young vandals (ages 3 and 4). What do I want? A trustworthy man filled with a lust for life who is interested in getting to know two little brats as well as their attractive mother.

As a woman of 43 with a son of 4, I wouldn't imagine there'd be many single males out there waiting to hear from me. Or am I wrong? If so, then I'd love to hear from you.

Which man between 35 and 40 would like to live and work in an Arab country together with a woman of 36 and child of 6?

Which doctor would like to get to know a nurse and her 2-year-old son better? Interests: spiritual growth, natural health care and enjoying the finer things in life.

Busy mother, 37, with son of 8 seeks enterprising man only for weekends.

Woman, 29, with son (1) seeks after previous disappointment the IDEAL MAN. I am independent, critical, stubborn and opinionated but am also vulnerable and ready to share. In order to grow I need room, rest and lots of love. I would like to meet an emancipated man who is mature, looks good, and can take the occasional setback.

Which man dares to stand in front of the bow of this 35-year-old archeress with three exuberant little 'fans' in the grandstand?

Which man would like to be part of this picture? A Christian family with three kids still going to school, a dog and a woman age 33 who is financially secure but who often feels lonely and would like a relation based on honesty and integrity.

Woman of 34, divorced, three kids, would like to meet a man. Being by myself, on my own, is getting to be more and more difficult, especially with December and the holiday season right around the corner.

I'm going to do this just to see what happens. Woman with two spontaneous kids age 8 and 10 would like to meet honourable man who is aware of what is happening around him and blessed with common sense and a warm heart which may have room for us as well.

Together with my two kids I've built up a life where we all feel pretty good. Still I miss the warmth, support and comradeship that a man can offer. Therefore I would like to meet a man.

A careful person . . . that I am, a woman of 35. But I am also daring and now that it's going good for me again, I would like to meet a man. I think it's important you know that I have a wonderful daughter and a very good job.

Opinionated, independent woman, 37, with a daughter and a good position, seeks a man with guts, around the same age, to form a united 'home' front. Do you enjoy your work? Are you unconventional? Would you also like to have another child? Then write this 'one-man-woman'.

Finally we come to those women who aren't already mothers but are looking to become so.

I have chosen to have a child all on my own. Is there a man who will help me? I'm a woman, 29, not lesbian, who awaits your answer.

I am a woman, 32, with a part-time job. I want a child and seek a man who is willing to be the donor. I intend to bear the full resposibility for that child but would like the father to stay in touch with the child.

I'm a woman who would like to have a child and seek an understanding man (35–45) who would not mind being a donor or – if it should work out even better than expected – being a (weekend) father.

It's fine and wonderful to have a child together.
But having a child on your own is also possible. I
am a woman of 38 who would like to have a child.
Which man, homosexual or heterosexual, would
like to be the father and perhaps also be(come) a
comrade for life? The exact arrangement to be
mutually agreed: weekend father; more than that;
less than that?

Woman, 36, would like to have a child. In order to
avoid anonymity I am approaching the future
donor in this fashion so that he, if he so desires,
can share in the responsibilities of being a parent.

Which hetero or homosexual man would like to be
the biological father of my child? The exact father
role to be negotiated.

CHAPTER 4 ■■■

Man seeks Man?

If only Adam could be here now, what would he think?

Come to think of it, what would have happened if God had been a little less inventive – after all, it was His day off – and had simply answered Adam's prayers with – another Adam! Sort of like Adam, Part II, a follow-up to God's earlier hit success. The two Adams would have shaken hands, gone camel riding a couple of times and that would have been it. No apple. No Paradise Lost. No John Milton or Cain or Abel. No floods, no famines, no wars. No Yo-Yos or Big Macs.

Yes, life would have been fairly dull if God had not been so creative – or is that mischievous? – and given us Eve, the original earth mother. But some men think they can still have more fun with their fellow Adams. The ads that follow have been assigned to this section rather than an earlier one because the choice of an Adam for his own likeness remains the overriding factor.

Although men are often accused of

93

being interested in only one thing, these ads prove that this simply isn't so. The men here enjoy a whole range of activities – with sport a high priority. Still, sex must play some small role in these relationships? How else would this group keep getting larger and larger?

In any event, Man the Hunter has also become Man the Hunted. Perhaps in so doing, he has come to understand himself – as well as Eve – a little better.

▼▼▼▼▼▼

A lot of men looking for other men choose to be extremely philosophical and poetic – as the following ads show.

Man of 29 seeks a male friend to live together on my houseboat. I am crazy about animals and have six cats and a dog. I am fairly simple, not the type who goes out much, and am neither good-looking nor ugly. I promise you nothing but am open to everything. What you look like is not so important as long as we can mean something for each other, which is far more valuable.

Every man has his own cross. Mine is that I can't find a friend. I am a man of 28, quick to grasp what's going on, more of a doer than a talker but sometimes 'oh so lazy'. I am looking for a man with a great deal of warmth and a sense of humour, who is reliable and yet interesting to be with. Oh how the clichés come, one after the other! More than anything else he must have 'IT', if you know what I mean.

Quiet man, 28, thin and modern, seeks the same in a black monogamous friend for a first-class black-white relationship.

Sometimes I'm a homo then again gay, stupid and smart, poor and rich, good-looking and repulsive, old and young, joyful and miserable, impotent and potent, serious and a bit touched. To make a long story short: a laugh and a tear. Which loving, faithful and honest masculine homo would like to take a place alongside of me?

For the journey to the end of the night one lantern is not enough. That is why I am seeking a male friend. I am 48, male and active. He is younger, not pansy-ish and someone I can talk and relate to.

I'll try again. Sometimes I wonder to myself: am I really homosexual? I do not feel at home in bars. I do not make a distinction between masculine and effeminate and I do not care for anal contact. Most of the time I fall for guys younger than myself, not pansy-ish, trim, attractive and with whom I can have a halfway decent conversation. Whoever can appreciate the artificiality of this kind of attempt (and future meeting) and who does not expect to find the 'needle in the haystack' should write me.

Sometimes the big, bad world is too much for me, a homo man of 28. I am looking for a smart, creative friend with an appreciation for art who is able to stand on his own two feet.

I seek a loving, intelligent and monogamous man of around 30 who is not afraid to have a deep relation with me, a man of 34, stubborn but soft with a caressing factor of 9 on a scale of 10.

Will you accompany me on my trip through life? I find myself now in the land of Yin and Yang. Who knows where our journey might take us further?

I can only think of the following words because I'm stoned out of my mind. But I'm no pothead. I'm gay, 28, blond, with eyes and a body to match. I want a male friend who will stand by me and who has good qualities.

You are either married . . . or not, don't like gay because you are masculine in your own way, have work and come from a good background. You are prepared to believe in a man and know what that is worth.

Teacher, 45, active in the church, seeks a male friend of same age or younger with same ecumenical disposition. I am not interested in park and sauna but in a different way of relating to each other.

Attractive man seeks another well-built man for a long time or for always.

Man of 22 seeks a well-to-do individual who, like myself, likes cashmere sweaters and linen suits. He also should know how to talk with conviction about Ralph Lauren, Bond Street, Gogol, Moustaki, Hayden, solitude and bisexuality.

Homo not known within usual homo circles would like to meet a shy young homo. A beginner is no problem. I am financially independent and have a large house with a beautiful garden and a very warm kitchen.

I want a TATTOO – but then a very good one. Which man knows something about this and can help me over a threshold while building up a friendship with a well-built, bisexual, 28-year-old motorcyclist?

Divorced bisexual man in his forties, weekend father, seeks masculine guy up to 45 to share a beer down at the pub. Write me, especially if you've never done that before.

Gay seeks Gay! The first party: blond, own house, bicycles and active with gay rights. The second party: interest in a monogamous relation, not fat and willing to write to . . .

DEAR READERS! Will you please cut out this personal and give it to a man between 25 and 40 who thinks he has enough good qualities that he doesn't have to advertise in order to meet someone. I am a man of 30 who is of the same opinion but doesn't want to wait for an accidental meeting.

According to me there aren't any long-haired homos with flair left who have the guts to arrange a meeting. We are all too afraid! And we're always thinking about sex. But why? Don't you think we should sit down and examine this closer?

Man of 58 is looking for a younger male FRIEND who enjoys classical music and would like to accompany him to concert halls. Preferably a man who doesn't hang out in the gay bar scene any more.

My name is John and I am a lawyer, thus not very wealthy. I live in a simple house in a peaceful neighbourhood and I do judo and play the piano. I am looking for a loving, male friend and preferably someone brown-skinned because, in general, brown-skinned people seem to be more friendly than white people.

' . . . two men learn to trust each other so completely that there's no fear and they experience and share everything in the flesh and the spirit'. (Isherwood). Who would like to strive together with me towards this?

Man seeks man. I'm a man, 24, a hundred per cent butch, with a good job in the business world. I don't enjoy the bar scene but do enjoy surfing, sailing, gardening, doing chores around the house and camping. I have many friends and am never alone or feel lonely but still I miss that one special guy who is about my age, is manly, and who would like to work towards a solid friendship so that we eventually could love each other in a natural fashion. Please tell me everything about yourself . . . your work, school, hobbies and so forth. If you have a problem with writing or maybe with your parents, that's okay. Let me know how I can reach you. No matter how difficult it may seem, I'll get through to you, somehow.

Dreaming of a blond young man, keeping an eye out for the dream-boat guy rippling with muscles, waiting for your Dream Prince and then ever so often grabbing whatever body is available so as to release your anxiety. And then, after all the promises and beautiful words and good intentions, seeing that 'relationship' fall apart because you still don't know what you want. Or who you want. So back to the Dream Prince. Does it always work out that way? I'm a man of 34 who has given up on bars with their superficiality and hungry looks and want a friend to share my life with on the basis of mutual respect, love and faithfulness so as to make life a lot richer and fuller than it already is.

I'm a divorced man, 33, bisexual, who is looking for a male friend. Why this ad? Because many lose interest when they find out about my kids and my desire to spend time with them, too. I am looking for a guy, homo or bisexual, who believes friendship to be: accepting each other for what you are; supporting each other; having fun; being serious; not saying anything when necessary; not being demanding or laying claim to each other; having respect for each other; learning to love each other truly; and making love the way it should, with everything and anything.

I'm not a copywriter so don't expect much with this ad. Besides, I don't want half of England to wind up in my mailbox . . . just the letter from the man whom I desire to meet. I'm a man who is looking for a man in order to have some fun together.

And then again we come to those 'short but sweet' ads – which, quite frankly, say it all. So who needs more?

I am a homo who has had it with one-night stands. I am curious.

Gay man seeks gay man.

Homo seeks trustworthy friend for warm relationship

I was very moved by the movie *AMADEUS*. Man seeks manly and sensitive friend with plans for a winter vacation.

Fun guy is looking for like-minded guys for friendship.

After 'Man's Lib' now 'real' man friendship. Man seeks (bisexual) boyfriend.

Man is looking for male friend in order to eat, sleep and wake up together. Which blond dream prince will come to kiss me in my sleep?

Attractive blond guy, very hairy, seeks a male friend: black, white, fat or thin.

Man desires long-running adventure with versatile young man.

Brother (33) is looking for a younger brother, ages 18 to 26, for a warm, imaginative and loving friendship. Write to your Big Brother.

Medicine man, 26, free of viruses, humanistic conservative, seeks a constant factor in the way of a virile, well-built young man with healthy character.

Good-looking guy of 42 would like to meet a sombre, conservative man, age 50 to 65, who is corpulent and enjoys wearing suits.

Male steward with airlines seeks a serious, manly friend for friendship vacation, going out and a relation(?). If you want more than just one night, then write.

Man, 48, seeks spontaneous male friend between 30 and 40 for serious relation. Purpose: to set up house-keeping. No pansies, please.

Male bear of 30 has pot of honey for male teddy.

I don't care if I lose the lottery so long as I win you. You are a young man, 16 to 25. I am a man of 36 with a place in his heart and house for you.

Purchase of a sail boat on a 50-50 basis is what I would like most. That is why I'm looking for a fellow homo who enjoys fighting the water and the wind. Good-looking guys are also welcome as members of the crew.

Beautiful blond guy seeks deliciously dark guy.

Man, 47, misses the most important thing in his life, namely, a good-looking masculine guy who he can love with all his heart.

'Magnum' type age 32 seeks contact with younger blond men.

Are you looking for homos too where you can drink coffee or wine? And without sex? Then write me.

Man with private swimming pool and sauna is looking for male friend(s) to enjoy a relaxed weekend together.

Which homosexual man up to the age of 45 would like to spend five days visiting all the cathedrals in south England by auto with a homo of 45?

Young man seeks gentleman who is willing to help him. I do not expect something for nothing.

Man with time-demanding job seeks well-hung friend with moustache.

Man of 34 seeks a smart guy for a durable and exclusive relationship. Ugly monsters and clowns need not apply.

Male professor willing to give remedial lessons to recalcitrant male(s).

To tell you the truth, I've had it with this loveless, hypocritical world. But I haven't given up hope for a little warmth for two. Homo male, 59.

Ahaaaaaaaa! The charming prince on his white charger? Both are welcome! Man is willing to open doors for you which have long remained closed. Those without chargers may also respond.

Soldier, 48, seeks a (much) younger male friend for a monogamous relation.

Homosexual businessman with a summer house in Spain desires well-built and well-hung manly and athletic man for friendship, for a relation, or for 'every now and then'.

Young man seeks male friend to love and to give and receive. Monogamous friendship . . . does that still exist?

'Young and Gay' . . . who knows, this just might be the way! Man seeks his 'one and only' who enjoys art and opera.

Man of 50, a late bloomer, youthful in appearance and spirit, is looking for a man to help him bloom.

Hello BLACK friend! Blond guy with fantastic body is looking for YOU!

Other men, of course, are very much interested in sex, and do not hold back from hinting at it or saying it straight out. After all, boys will be boys . . . and men will be men. Perhaps even more so when they are looking for other men.

WANTED: intelligent, tender male dish for endless love-making, talking, laughing and being still. Wanted by a youthful guy of 41.

Homo love can be a pleasant adventure for a man who doesn't wish to limit his lusts and fantasies.

Recently I saw a boy scout . . . but he had his hands full! How about you?

I would love to come into contact with a married man around 40. Someone who besides making love with his wife would enjoy getting it on with a good-looking guy of 30. We would be careful, of course, but still passionate!

Man seeks man for sex, love and to plan the future.

John, 42, seeks a male Negro who is sensitive around the nipples.

Man, 35, homo, seeks stability in life through a steady relation, yet with the freedom to fool around on the side every now and then.

Field-hockey player would like to try it once with a fun guy wearing corduroy pants.

Good-looking dude seeks good-looking dude for mutually satisfying massages.

Man, 52, homo, is still looking for a young guy up to 27. Last time I didn't get a reaction. Only making love and safe sex wanted. If you come from a great distance, I'll reimburse your travel costs.

White man seeks black man for sex contact.

'Part-time Lover' wanted. Man of 27 with steady relation seeks safe male partner for love-making on the side.

Greek love: which uncertain and hesitant young man would like some help from an experienced man to cross the threshold into the Promised Land of homo-erotica?

HOMO ADULTERY? Man would like to get it on with men between 18 and 37 without his regular male partner knowing about it.

Fat, bisexual man seeks student for regular hygienic sex contact.

Which young man in a pajama would like to climb up on my lap? I read and caress very nicely. You are angry at your parents and are crazy about sex and sex books. I would like to please you in every way possible.

Friendly kind of guy of 45 seeks male friend between 30 and 45 for both in and out of bed.

Nothing ventured, nothing gained. I'm a man looking for another man for, in the first place, to make wild and passionate love.

Man would enjoy exchanging erotic correspondence with other men.

Duo seeks homo pairs for friendship and physical pleasure.

What I expect of friendship is that it be fine to wake up together. Man of 46 seeks man up to 40 in order to go 'our' own way, together.

Are you gay and would you like to make love with me and stick around for breakfast afterwards? I'm a man of 35; relation is not completely ruled out. I enjoy tenderness during love-making and hope that you are warm but not too clinging. Please, no S&M and no thrill-seekers.

I am a left-wing lad and a Lennon fan. I'm looking for a boyfriend to talk to and to get it on with.

Is there a gay man out there who is prepared to literally expose himself? I want to see it! I want to draw it! And I want to make love to you and be your friend! I am a male artist in his thirties.

Gay man seeks gay man for friendship. I love to go out, travel, reading, my work and sex.

Man seeks homo sex in exchange for room with balcony.

Heteros are not the only ones who enjoy getting 'slap' happy. For those who like their sex with a bit more bite to it, the following personals may exude some appeal.

Male homo who has never advertised before would like to meet a man who may be shy but is not afraid to sexually experiment. Someone who would find it exciting to give or receive a nice healthy slap.

Attractive man seeks good-looking guy dressed in a classy suit who is willing to spank my (naked) ass.

Submissive, virile man seeks stylish dominant man.

Man is looking for a guy who could use a couple of hard whacks across his naughty bottom.

Man, on the surface a man but underneath a submissive woman, would like a sex relation with a dominant foreign male.

Cold weather and sweaty, glistening buttocks. Which guy would like to have his behind treated to an old-fashioned 'handling' on occasion?

FF-HOMO by the name of Jack, passive, seeks active FF-er, experienced or inexperienced, for the dark evenings on the horizon.

Homo, FF enthusiast, seeks energetic (young) man. FF IS SAFE. I am 38, tall and available. If you are ACTIVE, not fat and old and all dried up, with short fingernails and supple wrists, then you are most WELCOME!

From the world of abbreviations such as S&M and FF it is not too far to the world of kinks. And fetish. And the plain old unusual.

I'm a homo who would like to watch while you are busy with yourself. Which young man also gets excited by just thinking of this?

Man would like to meet exhibitionistic young man around 20.

Male homo and fetishist is crazy about shoes (size 42). Which young guy has a pair of beat-up Nikes to give, lend or trade? (Other brand of boots OK.)

Discreet, passive man of 36 seeks pervert between 45 and 65.

Respectable guy, bisexual, foot fetish, seeks man between 18 and 35 for foot treatments during the day. Preferably well-taken-care-of feet so that I can take even better care of them in the future. If you answer, you'll have no regrets, I promise.

Male homo requests examination by homosexual doctor.

Adonis would like to pose for an (amateur) photographer who might also like to pose as well.

Playing with yourself is even more fun if you know someone is watching. I (homo, 36) am exactly that someone.

Others simply express an interest in leather. Or uniforms. And those who are prone to wear such.

Active hobbyist in leather motorcycle jackets, rubber boots and rainwear would like to meet motorcyclists – preferably with Harley Davidsons – and men in uniform.

Man of 25 seeks soldier to have some fun behind the dunes at the beach.

WANTED: Heterosexual, bisexual or homosexual shepherd who would enjoy having his beat-up leather pants snuffled by this homo sheep.

Man of 34 seeks serious friend. Preference: policeman, soldier or motorcyclist.

Blond LEATHER BOY seeks fellow soul-mates who have a lot to offer with respect to rough sex and golden showers.

Softie would like to meet a man in uniform.
Absolute discretion assured.

Man of 43 seeks a man between 30 and 55.
Preferably someone a bit butch. Say, Army or even
Air Force. Are you muscular and well hung?
Doesn't matter whether you're married or single,
so long as you got what it takes.

I'm not young any more and I'm not good-looking.
Still, I could get off on the warmth of a vital, young
man. Preferably someone in uniform.

Long fingernails, a man, and leather. This is the
combination I seek in their proper order. I am 34,
male and gay and wonder where I'm going to find
you?

Which military man or police officer would like me
to be his most willing of slaves? I'm a man of 36.

Two men, 32 and 36, seek contact with police
agents, marines and military personnel. Discretion
assured.

For those who are more action-minded, there's
always sport – especially body building and
marathons.

Man in possession of body building/fitness
equipment and training area would like to come in
contact with men in order to train.

Man seeks male partner who is not interested in usual sex play but does enjoy physical contact such as wrestling and massage.

Man, 50, seeks younger friend for massage. I run marathons and run every day.

Man seeks another male to help him get over his fear of physical activity such as sport, fighting, wrestling, etc.

Man would like to make it with a body builder.

Which good-looking and muscular guy (maybe a body builder, what do you think?) can hold his breath real long and finds this as exciting as I do?

Bisexual man seeks a homosexual/bisexual man who is willing to go on a marathon with him and, who knows, continue running on into the sunset.

Red-haired guy is looking for a well-developed body builder to do some heavy-duty lifting together as well as push-ups. Preferably someone who knows all the 'ins' and 'outs'.

▼▼▼▼▼▼

Do you believe in mixing business with pleasure? Some guys do.

Homo, 52, with a lot of free time on his hands, seeks a male friend with his own business who could use some help.

Homo of 30 seeks man, 20–35, who besides a
steady relation dares to start up a pet shop (exotic
animals) with him.

Bisexual man of 31 seeks man with pioneer spirit
and performance-oriented to set up an agrarian
company in northern France. He should have an
interest in sheep and possess some capital. The
purpose is a partnership.

Finally, there are those men who are still looking to 'come out of the closet' – or for 'daddies'
willing to lend a helping hand.

Shy young man of 24 would like to discover the
sensuality of homo sex but is afraid of AIDS.
Which older man is willing to help me cross this
hurdle?

Which young man is willing to have me as sort of a
father and a friend (sugar daddy?)? Divorced man
of 45 would like to mean a lot to you!

Better late than never. Teacher, 29, homosexual, is looking for his first real boyfriend. Preferably a bit younger. I'm not quite yet ready to start living together, but I'm willing to try (almost) everything else.

Inexperienced man would like to meet an equally inexperienced man. I am 31, bisexual, passive, open-minded, intelligent, successful from the standpoint of society, exhibitionistic and (mildly) masochistic. You are the same but dominant, able to see things in relation to each other, imaginative and (mildly) sadistic. Goal: to examine each other sexually as friends, later for a more regular contact. Afraid? Shy? Yes, so am I.

Naughty, perverse son of 27 is looking for a loving but strict daddy, 40 to 60 years old, for friendship, sex and a little discipline. Skin colour is not important so long as he is not narrow-minded.

Young man seeks a MENTOR. It would seem not to be such a crazy idea to meet someone with more (life) experience because I myself don't view life as without having problems. I am 22, homosexual, a student, have a good character and expect you to share this last important trait.

Executive male aged 55 seeks male friend for weekends and vacations. Age from 25 years on up. Preferably for a father-son relationship with someone with an Asiatic background. But other possibilities are not excluded.

I have just discovered that I am homosexual. But I have also decided not to even begin with the whole homo and bar scene. Rather, I would like to build up a relation with someone who is willing to take the trouble and effort to make an investment in an honest and hopefully worthwhile future.

Stepfather seeks a stepson.

CHAPTER 5 ▪

Many men cannot understand why a woman would want a woman. Most of them believe themselves to be 'God's gift to women' when, as we all know, the reverse is actually true.

Many reasons have been given as to why a woman would choose a woman (over a man). A number of them regard it as a 'reaction' to man's tyranny. His drinking, his lies, his running around until all hours of the night. His general untrustworthiness and overriding unfaithfulness. Other theories, more general in tone, explain this preference of female for female to be a product of blurred sexual identities and the disintegration of traditional society along with its values. And perhaps these theories – and their theorists – are right to a degree. After all, the sociologists have to do something with all their free time.

But there is one theory which says: 'Some women simply prefer women'. No soul-searching, no psychoanalyzing, no society-in-transition. Quite simply, no nothing.

Perhaps, in this case, the simplest explanation is the best one of all.

WOMAN SEEKS WOMAN

Whatever the case may be, there is the case of woman preferring woman.

▼▼▼▼▼▼

If anyone can be 'short and sweet' it's got to be a woman. Many of the ads to follow are just that – others are a bit longer. But, all together, they should paint a picture as colourful as the women behind them.

I seek warmth and erotic feelings. I experience this more with women than with men. Which woman recognizes this in herself and wishes to share my feelings. I am a woman of 22.

Woman seeks woman to love.

Attractive woman seeks a girlfriend to stroll along the beach and through the forests, to gossip with and to laugh over a beer, to cry with and to make love to. If you want this, too, then write to me.

I am a girl of 22 who would enjoy getting it on with another woman.

LESBIAN: I would love to become intimate and fall in love with someone who does not mind that I smoke and drink and who doesn't get carried away with sport and sex. I am 45 and am looking for something special: freedom and growing old together.

Woman of 35 with daughter age 2 seeks exciting woman for a love relation.

As a pretty girl of 18 I only run into guys at the disco. But that is not who I am looking for. I seek a loving, spontaneous girlfriend who also wants to be part of something different.

Woman wants a pretty, wild woman.

I am a woman of 40, divorced, without children and just back from Switzerland. I am looking for a lesbian woman. I enjoy warmth, openness, tenderness, nature, music, art, travel, mountains, beaches . . . yes, everything!

A good-looking gal would love to make love to other gals.

LESBIAN WOMAN SEEKS DREAM PRINCESS? Offered: heavy dose of love of life, optimism and ambition (both in work and in personal life). Wanted: a woman who has both feet firmly planted on the ground and does not keep waiting for a dream to come along.

Married bisexual woman of 30 is missing something in her life. Are you a married woman and also looking for a warm relation? Perhaps we can complement each other and make our lives complete.

Solidly built woman would like to romp around (wrestle) in private with another woman.

Lesbian woman, 39, would like to have a child but does not look forward to doing this all on her own. Which woman is willing to take on this challenge and adventure together with me?

Woman desires woman to go to nudist beach on weekends. Suggestions also welcome as to other possibilities.

In short, I am a woman who is very sweet and attractive but that doesn't matter much to me. What does matter is tenderness and being able to snuggle up against another woman.

Woman of 25 seeks another woman in order to do everything together.

The 'hetero' state of being is fed to everyone with a spoon from the time they are a little baby. Which woman would like to find out what 'lesbian love' is all about?

Attractive bisexual girl, not exactly 'lonely' but feeling alone among all the heteros, seeks girlfriend.

I am a 21-year-old woman, loving, vulnerable, uncertain, honest, direct and open and I am seeking my dearest girlfriend.

Very feminine woman of 35 seeks a masculine woman of 40 for a mutually satisfying erotic relation. By the way, seduction is more important than the actual sex itself, no?

Two lesbian women would like to meet equally attractive women for . . . Well, we'll wait and see.

Inexperienced lesbian, age 36, seeks serious girlfriend for a good chat and a bit of adventure.

Creative woman fashion designer seeks woman age 30 to 40 who, in addition to a steady relation, would be willing to start up a clothing company.

Lesbian alcoholic seeks the same in order to solve our problems while having some fun at the same time.

Woman seeks woman to make love to and travel around the world with.

Lesbian woman seeks woman to talk with and to make love with and to go on vacation with on a 50/50 basis. Key words: cultured, discreet, mystical, camping/de luxe hotels/India? Travel around Spain? Florence?

Woman, 34, seeks another woman for massage, eventually to make love with. Hobbies: alternative medicine, astrology and making wine (drinking, too!)

Come bring me your softness. I'll give you my sweetness. Young woman seeks woman unto myself.

Woman seeks loving woman to talk, to cry and to laugh.

Lesbian seeks one or maybe even two girlfriends to solve the problem of an empty bed.

Single and free woman who wishes to stay that way seeks adventure and excitement with older woman.

Hippy gal seeks hippy girlfriend for a serious relation.

I am looking for my spiritual twin. I believe in losing oneself and growing with the help of another. Freed from conventions. Not afraid to cut yourself loose. If you are a mature woman of 30, then this woman would like to hear from you, especially if you answer to Pisces.

Cat-loving and liquorice-eating woman seeks the same in a lesbian partner.

American lesbian writer, 40, visiting for one year, is looking for friends for fun evenings out.

Woman seeks woman to make purple from the colours blue and red.

Bisexual woman seeks girlfriend with an interest for soft S/M.

It's getting colder and darker outside. That's why I'm looking for some lady friends to keep it nice and warm here inside. Woman, 33.

Lesbian, 36, seeks serious partner. Not bisexual.

Lesbian woman seeks contact with women for spiritual and physical intimacy. I am a woman who is beginning a new phase in my life. I am looking for a woman who is willing to live together in a spirit of harmony.

We are two women who are good friends, early thirties, and are a bit nonchalant, a bit smart, a bit gifted for business and a bit soft when it comes to love. We are looking for women who are 'a bit' like us, especially when it comes to that last thing. Or do you prefer the 'lesbian scene'? Give yourself that little 'bit' of encouragement and write us. Everyone who does so will be treated with discretion. Even we found this ad to be 'a bit' too much!

123

I'd like to have some fun. Which lesbian bisexual yuppie does too?

Woman of 40 with all the necessary life experience behind her still has a place in her life and in her nest for friendship and an intimate relation with a somewhat younger woman.

WOMAN, elegant and well-built, willing to play the GIGOLO in fantasies of other WOMEN.

Older lesbian woman seeks contact with refined elderly lesbian.

Now that both the work and the kids are out of the way, time for myself. I spend hours on end seldom feeling bored and feeling alone, but now I want to feel complete by expanding my contacts. How? A poem, a card, a letter. Maybe later on a telephone call or a dinner together. I'm not quite ready for a (steady) relation. I am 35 and lesbian and waiting to hear from you, whoever you are.

CHANNEL 6 ████

Consume, consume, consume.

That's all we ever seem to do nowadays. French fries . . . in three different sizes. Ice cream . . . in thirty different flavours. Automobiles . . . in a hundred different models. We consume them all, along with barbeque sets and mobile homes and videos and windsurfing boards . . . the list is endless. Doesn't it make sense, then, in a consumer's society, that people have started to consume – what else? – other people!

Two who want to be three. Three who want to be four. Four who want to be . . . Some people are never satisfied, swinging this way and that way. Left, right, north, south, people are eating each other up, with and without ketchup.

Perhaps what these people, and others less visible and expressive in their desires, need is a third sex. Yes, a THIRD sex. In order to bring into play a new balance, a new harmony, a new sense of order. Now most people must choose either A or B or a little bit of both. But what if there

125

was a real THIRD choice . . . a third sex? To the equations of A + B and B + A would be added the provocative possibilities of A + C and C + B. Wouldn't that make life a little more interesting?

Consume, consume, consume?

Mmmmmm. Delicious French fries. And delicious people.

▼▼▼▼▼▼

The first group are guys and gals, usually married, looking for a third party. Perhaps to have a party. Sometimes they prefer a man.

You might find it to be a bit strange but we are a happily married couple in our forties who sometimes find it fun to have a man join us. If you are sympathetic and spontaneous, brown or white, hetero or bisexual and think you would enjoy being part of our 'trio', then join us now because it gets dark mighty fast nowadays outside.

THREE-IN-ONE-POT: fun couple; him, jazz musician and upbeat; her, teacher and even more upbeat; middle forties; looking for a witty guy with a beautiful body for some additional pleasure.

Married couple, both 33, looking for fun guy, not bi, preferably sterilized.

Extravagant woman and young man are looking to do a few impulsive things with a spontaneous young man.

126

Hungry couple is looking for a sweet slave.

BLACK, BROWN or WHITE bisexual man wanted by a good-looking pair, she in her mid-thirties, he in his early forties, with an interesting job and a fine house and home. Purpose: warmth, humour and erotic pleasure.

Which man (preferably sterilized) around 45 would like to experience friendship and erotic contacts with a married couple who are not yet tired of each other.

I am a man of 35 who is looking for another man (not homosexual; a bit bisexual would be best) for my wife and myself.

But most of the time they prefer a woman.

Charming heterosexual couple – both around 45 – are looking for a nice girlfriend who loves making love. A touch of 'bi–' would not be a disaster!

Inquisitive couple, desire uncomplicated woman for intimate relationship.

She is 23, he is 37 and they love each other many years already (although unmarried). They don't like pigeon holes, going to extremes or dishonesty. They do like nature, homeopathy and the pleasure that comes with being with somebody and for somebody. Which woman would like to share her life with them on an equal basis so that the three of them may discover together just how wonderful and full of love life can be every single day?

Young woman and man would like to 'team up' with a woman.

For some time we have wanted to do something exciting together with a mutual girlfriend. Are you a woman and do you feel the same way? Then tell us which one of us you would first like to go out to lunch with. The woman is just under 50 and the man just past 50.

A man and a woman form a pair
And are as happy as two hares,
But to be quite frank and candidly said,
They'd love to find a bisexual woman in their bed.

Modern, hip married couple seek modern, hip woman for a modern and very hip friendship.

Which woman would like to join us for a warm winter in front of the fireplace? Man is 40, woman is 37 and we enjoy art.

Attractive bisexual woman, 27 and married, would like to meet a similar-minded woman who would agree that a three-way relationship offers everything one might want in the way of a lasting and fine relationship.

I'm a woman with a preference for women. For many years I've had a male friend for whenever I needed him. If you are a woman who enjoys women a lot and likes men a bit, then maybe the three of us can work something out together. Thirty is good, forty is even better and you are still welcome if you're fifty.

CARPE DIEM! Woman, 34, bisexual, and guy, 33, heterosexual, are looking for (a) girlfriend(s).

We are a young couple with a weekend relationship and are looking for the woman who can make life for us a little more interesting in an uncomplicated fashion.

Woman, 22, is looking for a girlfriend to play and fool around together with a husband, age 48.

Two women to make love with one man. My husband is 45 and I'm 25. I'm African and am looking for a blond woman around 30.

Modern couple, both 29, seek young woman for friendship, going out (to eat) and for intimate weekends with us at home. We can understand if you should feel hesitant . . . but go ahead and try us, anyway.

Blond woman, 23, and athletic man, 34, seek a soft, erotic woman to be able to enjoy each other intensely. Do you want to make your fantasies reality? Then by all means, write us and see what happens.

Involuntarily childless couple would very much like to meet a woman willing to be a surrogate mother for us.

We are a man of 37 and a woman of 28 who are married and (in spite of that?!) love each other very much. We would like to share our future life with someone and have been thinking of a woman who also believes in fairness, comradeship, idealism and enjoys walking through nature, good music, sports, but also being lazy, eating . . . in short, everything that life has to offer.

Fun couple, both 23, would love to meet a bisexual girl for romantic evening.

Attractive couple, both 35, are looking for a free-thinking woman for an evening out, a game of Monopoly and erotic games for three, based on friendship and respect for each other.

Married couple (woman bisexual) have an extra room and would like to take care of a girl/woman from the age of 16 on up.

We are looking for a female friend. Woman is 44, guy is 57 and thin. We have a place in our hearts and our bed for a loving girlfriend.

Hello! We are looking for a bisexual woman up to the age of 35 in order to work towards a pleasurable contact. We are a married couple of 33 and 30 with two children.

Man, 48, seeks 3 to 4 girlfriends to have some fun together with a woman age 22. The more the merrier? You be the judge.

Next in line are all the (married) couples looking to spend some time with other (married) couples.

Married couple, middle thirties, seek another couple for swapping or four-way sex without jealousy.

Fun couple with broad interests seek another couple for friendship and partner exchange.

Attractive couple seeks couple for some hot evenings.

The Story of O. Fantasy or reality? Which couple is curious just like us (m/w 42) in finding out just how much can be true?

Couple, in their thirties, seek contact with another couple for some fun evenings at home playing cards, making a fondue and getting 'a little' intimate without getting carried away.

Couple seeks couple to get it on with.

Man and wife, bisexual, interested in classical music, art and literature, would like to meet a Japanese couple who have the same interests.

We don't have the slightest idea what we should put in here. Anyone who feels like contacting a married couple should just go ahead and do so.

Man, 27, and lady friend, 26, would like to make love with people other than just ourselves on occasion.

SHE and HE seek another SHE and HE for friendship and sex in a relaxed atmosphere.

We feel like two idiots here among all these beautiful and wonderful erudite people who are all looking for someone even more beautiful, more wonderful and so on and so on. We are a couple in our thirties who are looking for another couple who would enjoy having a few laughs and making love. Preferably not ugly and/or super fat but simply spontaneous and genuine.

Couple in their fifties desire couple in their sixties with modern ideas.

Married couple, happy together and forever young (40 and 38). Enjoy mind games, tennis games and sex games and seek a tender, tactful couple for some super-charged erotic evenings.

Couple, late thirties, do it without inhibitions and with pleasure. Because we believe that $2 + 2 =$ an evening full of fun, we are looking for another couple. Mathematical talent not required, only social talent.

You rarely run into real 'doers'. Nevertheless we would like to try to meet another couple who are as relaxed as we are when it comes to matters of importance.

Married couple, she 43, he 44. Although we don't have any experience per se, we don't really believe in husband and wife swaps. Therefore we are both going our separate ways in seeking a supplementary (and intimate) relationship. She would like a good-looking guy up to 45 to go out with, dancing, etc. He has his own company, is not much of a dancer, but would not mind going out with a woman between 25 and 40.

What about two guys looking for two gals? Do the guys in question have to hold each other's hand to go out on a date 'to hold hands'? Or is it a case of there being strength in numbers? Whatever the reason it still adds up to four.

Two bachelor friends (35 and 33) have decided to place an ad together but we couldn't quite agree as to what to put in. Both of us are looking for some female company. Women who like men, aren't bar types and who enjoy going out to the pub and going away on vacations. We enjoy eating good food, a few laughs, music and everything that life has to offer. We collect bad traits and would be more than happy to exchange them with somebody. Keep your photos; a long letter is much better!

Two male friends seek two women up to 32 to get us through the winter.

Two blokes are looking for two dames who enjoy getting out of the house. We could 'unbare' ourselves even further, but as they say: 'Another time, another place'.

Two good-looking guys, interested in the erotic and being a bit sociable, seek two attractive girlfriends for a no-holds-barred sex party.

Two ski instructors living in Austria would like to spend the holidays with two very sporty young ladies.

Two men, both 35, would like to play a few hands of strip poker but still require two female players. Who is ready to cut our deck?

Henry and Bill seek two birds for ski vacation.

Two brothers seek two women who are sisters or girlfriends. We have been bachelors long enough. John is a central heating mechanic with two right hands, lives at home, enjoys pop music, cooking, organizing parties and has character, is sensitive and easy-going. Peter, 27, a manager, enjoys modern/classical music, concerts, nature and is serious without being a bore and is sensitive. We are both always on the move and like to do odd jobs around the house. We both own cars, smoke but are not bar or Don Juan types. If this ad appeals to you, then send a letter and a photo. We can go out and see if we can make something of the future. Getting to know each other in a group of four is perhaps more fun and less frightening than with just two. Perhaps we will see you.

Magnum and Higgins would enjoy the company of two lively chicks.

Invitation for two women up to 35 for a Xmas dinner with two males. We offer you dinner with atmosphere, good conversation and, at the end of the evening, a game (Risk?). Wanted is some pleasant company with a sense of humour and a willingness to help clean up afterwards.

Ever so often doing 'it' with someone. Two attractive guys seek two fun gals who also would like to do something (else).

If two guys can do it, why not two gals?

Two free 'birds' fly ever so often to the theatre, cinema, museums, etc. Which two hopefully not bald eagles would like to fly along?

After a bit of hesitation we are finally ready! We are two girlfriends who are both looking for a man. I, Rita, enjoy a very full and 'rich' life and want a mate. The 'click' is very important to me. I, Nellie, am a very active woman who has managed on her own to make it this far but would still like a man at her side.

Margaret and Irene, both around 30, are free again! Hurrah! And are interested in meeting you! You too?

We are two girlfriends, 40 and 30, who are looking for the same in two guys for a LAT relation. Our positive characteristics: funny, loyal, honest and inventive. Our negative traits: opinionated, mercurial, lazy and sloppy.

Two women, both 30 and with a child of 4, seek two single guys up to 35 to go out with. We can see what happens after that.

WANTED: two princes on white horses. Lost: two slippers which fit two fun-to-be-with women ages 28 and 30.

Two girlfriends will be turning 29 in November. Which two guys would like to help us celebrate?

You can become richer by sharing your loneliness.
Two women would like to spend the holidays with
two men by making a fondue. Any other
suggestions?

Then there are those ads which go beyond two
looking for two. In all combinations. And for
whatever reasons.

Three government officials who really know how
to enjoy life – one of them 'attached' – have a few
free hours during the day which they would like to
spend with a woman who also knows what life has
to offer and isn't afraid to reach out and grab it. As
to how these free hours should be filled, we'll
simply have to figure that out.

Modern handsome and stylish couple are giving a
party at their mansion between the 4th and 9th of
August. To take place in a romantic and at times
even erotic atmosphere. Couples and single
women are cordially invited to respond.

137

Five women, all in their thirties, only meet other women. We want to meet some men. Now. To talk to, walk with and . . .

Which men and women up to 34 would dare join our little group? Aim: a few laughs. Evenings of carefree, voluntary group sex in a relaxed setting.

Four women would like to meet some men . . . to begin with, an evening with coffee and wine. Our ages range from 35 to 55 and one of us in particular would like to get married soon. You should be unattached spiritually, financially and physically (no Siamese twins, please) and well-dressed and clean. Lack of character leads to immediate disqualification.

Three energetic couples between 35 and 45 seek two or three other couples between 30 and 50 for weekends filled with amusement. Wanted: hedonistic, enterprising types who are extremely well-developed.

Three men seek three women for an (un)forgettable evening.

We are three women who know perfectly well what we don't want but where are the guys who will show us what we do want?

Brother (22) and sister (25) would like two or more 'beautiful people' to take care of us this coming Xmas.

To: all the guys who are in their thirties. Fact: all the women who respond to our ads have problems. Question: will the guys who have had more luck than us please explain to us the finer points?

Three tough broads would like to go out at least once with a bunch of wild guys.

Finally, there are those who leave the sexual side to someone else. Their quest is more serious, perhaps. Perhaps not. But they, too, want more than two.

Orwell wasn't completely right; you can still choose your own friends! And we are looking for a few new ones. Due to a long stay overseas, we (he 50, she 35, for both their second marriage) feel a bit isolated since coming back. Which persons can identify/sympathize with this situation and will write to us?

Small commune is looking for a woman. Key words: far-reaching friendship, spiritual growth and care and consideration for both the emotions and the practical side.

Two women would like to meet some others who would like to get together once every two months to rap about books. Good books are central to the discussion envisaged.

Towards a new psychiatry. Who would like to join me? I am a woman who herself uses meditation with an interest in psychiatry. I live with one young woman and two young men who need attention.

We are two women and a man living in a small village. Just the three of us? You, too? We would like to receive your comments, insights, whatever you may have to say. We could use your support.

Life community seeks contact with (young) people who would like to make their, our and the entire world more livable by seeking true love.

By this means we – homosexual and lesbian teachers – hope to come in contact with other like-minded colleagues who will help us fight against the hetero norm.

We are three unconventional and spiritual persons (two women and a man), in their thirties, who would like to expand their 'family unit' with a man, a woman or a couple. We live in the city in a big house and a big forest in back. Point of reference: caring for each other and working together while leaving room over for one's own (inner) development.

CHAPTER 7 ![]

The elderly.

Many of them have worked forty or more years to get where they are today. You can read it on their faces. You can read it even better on their bodies. More often than not, their hip joints ache, their vision is going and it takes all they have to walk down the hall and back. But they try. Yes, they try. And they sit in their flat or home for the elderly, composing ads and counting the days until . . . Until what? Until they get an answer. Or until they . . .

And yet the greatest joy that an older person can profess to is to say: 'I am vital.' But what does this mean? And why do you come across this word so often in the personals placed by the elderly?

First of all, vital comes from the word 'vita', the Latin word for 'life'. How wonderful it must be to speak about yourself in such a fashion! To say to 100 or 200 or even 500 thousand readers, many who may not care, 'I am alive, I am vital.'

But it also suggests something more, that the person in question is ready to 'give' life. Sex, perhaps? Maybe. Who knows? Does it really matter? For some it does, obviously. While for others life is life. And at that age, in this age, to utter 'I'm alive' is saying quite a mouthful.

▼▼▼▼▼▼

Some people talk of living too long. But life is always too short, especially for those who know 'how' to live it. Some of those – a few – are to be found on the following pages.

Lively, unconventional, vital woman, almost 70, independent (financially, too) and with a good job but without male companionship, seeks an intelligent male friend who enjoys biking, taking walks, going out, staying at home and making love.

Gentleman, 80, university-educated, would like to live together with a Christian lady.

Youthful 60-year-old businessman, single, seeks girlfriend, preferably a nudist.

Vital, youthful 60-year-old. A pastor and admirer of Pope John XXIII who can not afford to miss any longer the feminine component in his private life. Which tender and youthful woman can understand this? Purpose: candid exchange of ideas and feelings; release from taboos in our thinking and way of doing things; and learning to love each other as much as possible. I am an idealist and sensitive and an excellent cook. Skin colour and background are unimportant with a slight preference for Asiatic women. If you feel something 'click', then please respond. You won't be sorry. Even if we don't reach our paradise here on earth, a new friendship is always good!

There must be a widower between the ages of 58 and 63 somewhere who, just like me (widow, 59) doesn't know where or how we can find each other. We are certainly not too old, don't you agree?

Man of 70 seeks young man or a couple.

I am a man of 58, not rich, and enjoy going to flea markets, comradeship and my freedom. Which uncomplicated woman who believes that happiness is more important than money will get in touch with me?

I would like to meet a man who, like me, a woman of 55, is not happy with his marriage. I love classical music, nature and most of all happiness because then one's difficulties are easier to bear. If you're only after sex, I'd rather you didn't respond.

When he comes home our father misses the smell of meat simmering and everything associated with that: homeliness, friendship, companionship and so on. He also doesn't know what to do with his season ticket for two to the Concert Hall. Which woman might be interested?

Is there a young woman, age 25, who would like to come live with me (60-year-old retired tradesman) and do the cooking for both of us and some light housework? I can offer you (and your child) a free and carefree existence in pleasant surroundings. Your own room(s) and plenty of free time. We will have it good together, believe me.

Good-looking widow is looking for a single male as a life partner, around 70, with an auto, in order to begin a LAT relation and still enjoy life. He is a man of honour and must have style, presence and come from a good background. We may be both looking for the needle in the haystack but can go on breathing quietly, hopefully together.

Grandson seeks on behalf of his grandfather an old gentleman as a companion because grandpa can't handle being alone so well.

Single, divorced man of 60 seeks young woman to live with. You should love horses and be prepared to go riding or learn how to.

I am a man, alone, who has yet to find his one true love after sixty-five years on this planet. Romantic and vital, I am looking for a woman around 60 who would enjoy going abroad on occasion.

Which loving woman would like to get together with a widower, age 78, who has been alone for the past eight years and would like to make some plans for the coming holidays?

Pastor would like to be able to call himself a homo, but doesn't dare. I am 60 and need a male friend to talk to and laugh with.

Which man of around 60 doesn't want to give up his freedom but would still like a partner to go out with, to eat with and to spend some time at home with? Especially during the holidays. I am a 60-year-old woman and love animals.

Woman seeks loving man between 68 and 72.

Man in late fifties, divorced, previously active in the business world, presently suffering from a slight speech and walking impediment due to a stroke. I am looking for a woman/life companion to give life more colour and meaning.

Creative woman, 70 years young, seeks unusual girlfriend up to 80 for LAT.

Man, 75, has car, cannot drink, smoke or go to pubs. Feels himself to be totally isolated and lonely. Seeks single woman, age unimportant, preferably thin, for vacations, reunions and for staying at home, watching TV and giving each other warmth and love.

Retired detective seeks young and fun dame, not older than 59.

Businessman of 67 with presence but without pretentions seeks woman who is active and will help him with his work, take care of his house and who will add something to it as well. I travel regularly to Spain for my work. Age is unimportant; preferably between 45 and 55.

Woman of 57 seeks a man to share the rest of her life in harmony.

Widower, not young, not attractive and not sporty, seeks woman up to 60 for a non-platonic relationship in which anything can happen, but nothing has to.

Woman of 86 would like to come in contact with a man, woman or couple for bridge, Scrabble, Mah Jong or whatever in order to drive off the loneliness.

Which adventurous woman would like to travel across North Africa on a 50–50 basis with a 61-year-old man?

Man, 70, married, seeks lady friend for (ir)regular, intimate contact, age up to 75, discretion assured.

I feel so lonely. Who will make an invalid woman a little happy? Someone preferably with an auto and between 70 and 75.

I am looking for friendship with a man and woman up to age 40. A man who is big, dominant and bisexual and a woman who is loving and sweet. But other combinations are also okay. I would like to add to your pleasure but also don't mind watching and enjoying myself, too. I'm a man of 65.

We don't have that much time left. I'm a man of 60 and you're a woman between 50 and 58. Write me, quick!

Vital and single woman seeks serious man for fun, affection and love. Age 65–70. Preferably in possession of a phone and auto.

Woman, recently divorced seeks a many-sided man.

Girl of 16 seeks a good male friend between 58 and 65 for her grandmother.

I'm looking for a man up to 67 for my youthful and sexy-looking mother (61).

CHAPTER 8 ▮▮▮

Americans and Canadians, Polish and Hungarians, Africans and South Americans, Indians and Japanese . . . they all want to meet an Englishman! And many want to live and stay in the U.K. Why is that?

The Europeans cross the Channel in order to be able to practise the English they thought they learned in school. The Yanks come here to practise the English they never learned in school. And the Japanese come over to practise driving on the left-hand side, just like they do at home. Except this time at twice the speed and with cameras clicking.

And the Africans, the Arabs, the South Americans and the Indians? What do they want? Could it be the unbelievably beautiful sunny weather? The delicious exotic meals of kippers or pork sausages? Or is it simply the wild and passionate dancing in the streets that goes on deep into the night? No, these all play a role, of course, but are not the single most important factor. No, that is the residence permit. A simple stamp in a person's passport that has been known to put a smile on many a foreigner's face.

Most of the ads are in some form of the English language. Whether or not they are in the 'King's' English is something better left for the next King to worry about. Some would like you to come to them; others are already in England, enjoying kidney pies and the *Daily Mirror*. But they all have one very special thing in common.

They all want you.

▼▼▼▼▼▼

American gals have hit town! First time in Europe! Lots to see! Lots to do! If only we could find Mister Right! We know that you are out there but we don't know where, do you? Come on and introduce yourselves! Do you meet the following requirements: sense of humour, love to travel, dining out, music? Are you warm, a real go-getter and a good conversationalist? We know you are, so drop us a line and who knows?

Dutchman living in London desires to meet a lady.

African businessman seeks loving woman for friendship. Age not important but frankness and warmth are.

I am an Indian by birth and married three years to an Englishman. Many of my fellow countrywomen would also like to marry an Englishman. If you are interested, then please ask for further information.

Woman from Sri Lanka is looking for a man who would like to come and live in Sri Lanka.

If you like warm-blooded Latins and if you are a warm-blooded woman, then please write me. Don't forget a picture, okay?

Americans (300) working in Turkey (not military) would like to contact females interested in future meetings. Please send photo to . . .

I am a trustworthy man of 28 from Bangladesh who would like to build up a steady relation with a nice woman who is also interested in psychology, philosophy and who doesn't smoke or drink. Is there such a person?

Good-looking, honest and tender Australian man in London. Are you honest and pretty? Want to be my girlfriend?

Turkish man of 33 seeks British woman. Purpose: marriage.

Two Indian girls would like to correspond. Purpose: marriage.

Polish businessman would like to marry a British woman.

Egyptian, 32, regular job, honest, seeks lady for serious relation. Children are welcome.

American child specialist and 14-year-old daughter still require help integrating into British life. Required: instructions on cooking, shopping, homework and running the house. Patience, a smile and a sense of humour more important than ability.

Polish man living in USA wants to meet GIRL during visit to UK.

Young Russian woman, 31, already living a few years in UK, of Jewish extraction, desires contact with well-bred man.

Hello! I hope that by means of these few simple words I can find the man who will change my existence. Someone who will pamper me, protect me, let me see the world and yet answer my dearest dream – to have a family in England. I am a 35-year-old woman, charming and lady-like, from Poland, living here already for five years and blessed with a warm, beating heart and a most willing ear.

Eastern lover seeks adventurous woman for loving relationship.

East African woman would like to meet a man from a good background. Purpose: to live together, later marriage.

Man, 28, from Kurdistan. Living since 1984 in UK, political refugee, progressive thinker and studying law. I seek a progressive woman between 18 to 25 who can help me with everything.

Divorced man in South Africa would like to make contact with a woman to build towards a serious relation.

Australian and British men in Australia are seeking British birds (16–40) for friendship and marriage. Immigration possible.

Romantic South American woman seeks serious relation with a sympathetic man in a good financial position.

US businessman in Florida seeks (British) mother for his children, ages 10 and 11. Nice home. Will be in England next month.

American, male, university background, stranded in London, searching for a way in or a way out with a woman, 25 to 38, who also isn't exactly sure how it is or should be.

Businessmen looking for girls (Asian type) for marriage should write to . . .

Many of my girlfriends here in the Philippines would love to make the acquaintance of a charming British male. Information can be requested at . . .

Actually I'd like to have a fantastic relation, but they don't just fall out of the trees, do they? To begin with I want a woman between 27 to 35 to go to the show, dancing, concerts and for a love relationship in which each person values the other for who he or she is. I am an African from Cameroon and have a job and study part time.

Divorced Frenchman seeks woman up to 51 who can speak either French or English in order to build up a new life together.

Iranian seeks British/Arab/Iranian woman to marry.

If you are a young, independent woman of academic background and articulate in the English language, possessing poise, sensibility and, above all, a harmonious combination of anatomical and cerebral qualities, as well as having an affinity for Indian culture, then I, a male, 40, and a teacher with a similar background and disposition would love to hear from you.

WIFE: For Alaska Rural School Administrator. Wife should be nurse, teacher, etc. attractive, proportioned and between 25–35. Exchange letters/videos.

American, 44, plump, bald, cultured. Sold
business and retired early. Wants to travel, meet
new people and generally have a good time! Likes
music (heavy rock, classical), theatre, cinema,
travel, and romance. Would like to meet cultured
Englishwoman, 25–45, no ties, non-cigarette
smoker, as travel companion, friend, lover? Must
have young outlook on life and romantic nature.

Buon giorno! Classy Italian man, 43, seeks woman
for serious relation, love and tenderness.

African, 30, living in Freetown, Sierra Leone,
West Africa, good-looking, interested in travel,
music and movies, wants to correspond with a
British female.

Hello, my name is Peter. I'm a good-looking 25-
year-old engineer. My hobbies are flying, sailing,
skiing, dancing and travelling. I plan to travel to
Europe and would like an intelligent lady to show
me England. In return I offer to show you Canada.

Arab, 27, seeks woman between 22–32 with a
house, car and job.

Bulgarian architect, 44, speaks English, Italian and
German, would like to meet a British male.

Woman who can teach me English is urgently
requested. In return I offer you honesty,
friendship, Spanish lessons and maybe sex.

Italian, 24, married, living four years in UK, seeks
Italian and English girlfriends.

My girlfriend from South America, 32 and with three daughters in school, would like to meet an honourable Englishman who enjoys kids and is willing to build towards a new future.

New Zealander, late twenties, would like to correspond with attractive young lady, mid to late twenties. Please reply with photo.

Latin American woman, 35, sociologist, would like to meet a man in the UK. After corresponding in Spanish (or in English), we could meet this summer when I come to visit my married sister in England.

CHAPTER 9 ▬

DOG SEEKS . . .

Dog seeks . . .?

What's this, now?

As if it weren't bad enough with all these human Adams and Eves, trios and quartets, the elderly and foreigners!

But didn't you know that dogs are currently also 'doing it'?

What, you don't believe me?

Then turn the page and find out for yourself.

Woof, woof! My 19-year-old master is looking for a girlfriend, WOOF, someone who would like to go together with us on long walks. If you are, WOOF, not older than 25, then please write to, WOOF, . . .

The other day I was shuffling through the pile of papers on my desk. I thought I had gathered all the 'pretty personals' I had wanted to share with you. And I had, except for one.

There, at the very bottom of the pile, I found it. I confess; it was MINE! I had never sent it in to the paper, though. I had held on to it, afraid that if I sent it in, what I wanted would never come true.

But now I think it's safe to share my personal with you.

It reads:

> Writer
> without money . . . but with a book
> seeks
> reader
> without a book but with money.

This may be the end of the book and our 'contact' but contact ads are here

to stay. I hope you enjoyed yourself. I know I did.

Until the next time . . . don't just be PRETTY – be PERSONAL!